THE PATH OF LIGHT

THE PATH OF LIGHT

How Education Defeats Darkness

ANTON ANTHONY, ED.S, TH.D

Anton Anthony, Ed.S, Th.D

Contents

INTRODUCTION: THE JOURNEY FROM DARKNESS TO LIGHT

1	The Transformative Power of Education	10
2	The Universal Call from Darkness to Light: Lessons from World Religions	33
3	Jesus, The Great Teacher	42
4	Overcoming Ignorance and Prejudice	52
5	Serving Others: The Heart of True Education	64
6	Poverty, Addiction, and the Path to Enlightenment	77
7	Entrepreneurship as a Path to Light	98
8	Integrating Faith and Education	118
9	Preparing for the Future: Educating the Next Generation of Leaders	141
10	Vision for a Brighter World	162
11	Conclusion: The Everlasting Light of Knowledge and Service	186

References   191

About The Author 207
Contact The Author 209

Introduction: The Journey from Darkness to Light

> **PERSONAL ANECDOTE: MY JOURNEY AS AN EDUCATOR AND SPIRITUAL SEEKER**

From the outside, my life may seem like a straightforward path of success, but the journey was anything but ordinary. My name is Dr. Anton Anthony, Ed.S, Th.D, and this is my story of finding light through education and faith.

Growing up, I was an average student in high school with a love for basketball. Like many teenagers, I didn't have a clear sense of direction. College seemed like the next logical step, so I enrolled at Fort Valley State University. My college experience was typical, filled with studying, socializing, and participating in the latest trends. I followed the path that society laid out: study hard, get a degree, and hopefully make money. But despite graduating, I felt lost, with no true sense of purpose or direction.

After graduation, the advice was to continue my education to increase my earning potential. But this left me questioning my true calling. I realized that without a divine calling or an internal push, many of us are like ships without a compass. We often follow in our parents' footsteps if they had a clear path, but otherwise, we wander aimlessly.

Throughout my college years, I experienced a persistent, otherworldly feeling—a spiritual experience that hinted at something greater than myself. Yet, my flesh and worldly distractions kept me from fully embracing it. I was caught in the typical college cycle: drinking, getting high, partying, and following whatever trends came my way. This lifestyle blinded me to my true purpose.

The turning point came after I left college. I began to pray—not in the traditional sense, but through a meditative, contemplative prayer. In these moments of seeking something greater, I heard a small, still voice say, "You are a teacher." Initially, I didn't fully understand what it meant, but the certainty of the message was undeniable.

Despite having a business degree, I decided to pursue this calling. I enrolled in a Master of Arts in Teaching (MAT) program at Augusta State University in Augusta, Georgia. Completing the program in a year, I embarked on my journey as an educator. From my first interaction with students, I saw their eyes light up when they learned something new from me. My innovative and charismatic teaching style resonated with them, and I knew I had found my true path.

Throughout my career, I have served as a teacher, assistant principal, principal, and now, a human resource manager. My journey led me to found AA STEAM & Entrepreneurship Academy, a charter school dedicated to enlightening young minds through education and service. Though the school is not yet operational, I am confident it will be approved and will make a significant impact.

As a successful author with many years of experience in education, my journey is a testament to the transformative power of education and faith. This is just the beginning of the story I want to share with the world, a story of overcoming darkness through the light of knowledge and wisdom.

Purpose and Themes of the Book

THE MOTIVATION BEHIND WRITING THIS BOOK

The motivation for writing "The Path of Light: How Education Defeats Darkness" comes from a deep analysis of my own life, career, and extensive research. As an educator, I've witnessed firsthand the transformative power of education. More importantly, my faith has shown me that knowledge is a divine gift, a light that dispels the darkness of ignorance. The Bible says, "My people are destroyed for lack of knowledge" (Hosea 4:6, NIV), and this scripture has resonated with me throughout my journey.

Throughout my career, I've seen how education can uplift individuals and communities, providing opportunities that were previously out of reach. Research supports this, demonstrating that education is a key driver of social and economic mobility. According to a study by the Brookings Institution, higher educational attainment is associated with increased earning potential and better health outcomes . This book aims to share these insights and provide a roadmap for harnessing the power of education to overcome life's challenges.

Key Themes

1. **Education as Light**: This book explores how education serves as a beacon of light, illuminating minds and opening doors to new possibilities. It discusses how knowledge and wisdom can lead to personal and societal transformation.
2. **Wisdom and Service**: True wisdom is not just about acquiring knowledge but also about applying it to serve others. This theme highlights the importance of service in education, emphasizing how teaching children to help others can lead to a more compassionate and just world.
3. **Faith and Spiritual Growth**: Drawing on religious and biblical teachings and personal spiritual experiences, this book illustrates how faith can guide educational journeys. It underscores the belief that a relationship with God is the foundation of true knowledge and wisdom.
4. **Overcoming Ignorance**: Ignorance is a form of darkness that limits potential and perpetuates prejudice. This book examines how education can combat ignorance, fostering understanding, empathy, and social harmony.
5. **The Role of Educators**: Educators play a pivotal role in guiding students from darkness into light. This theme delves into the responsibilities and impact of teachers, showcasing stories of educators who have made significant differences in their students' lives.

What Readers Can Expect to Gain

Readers of "The Path of Light: How Education Defeats Darkness" can expect to gain:

- **Research-Based Evidence**: Supported by research, the book provides compelling evidence of how education can lead to better life outcomes, reduced poverty, and enhanced social cohesion.
- **Spiritual Enlightenment**: Readers will explore the deep connection between faith and education, understanding how spiritual growth can complement and enhance the quest for knowledge.
- **Tools for Overcoming Challenges**: The book equips readers with strategies to overcome ignorance and prejudice, encouraging them to seek understanding and embrace diversity.
- **Inspiration**: Through personal anecdotes and success stories, readers will be inspired to see the value of education and its transformative power.
- **Practical Insights**: The book offers practical advice for educators, parents, and policymakers on how to create educational environments that nurture wisdom, service, and faith.

By weaving together personal experiences, faith, and rigorous research, "The Path of Light: How Education Defeats Darkness" offers a powerful and timeless message. It aims to enlighten readers, helping them realize the potential of education to transform lives and bring about a brighter, more compassionate world.

The Metaphor of Light and Darkness

Explanation of Light as a Symbol of Knowledge, Wisdom, and Enlightenment

In many cultures and religious traditions, light is a powerful symbol representing knowledge, wisdom, and enlightenment. It signifies the clarity and understanding that comes with learning and spiritual growth. Throughout history, light has been associated with truth and the divine. In the Bible, light often symbolizes God's presence and guidance. For instance, in Psalm 119:105, it states, "Your word is a lamp to my feet and a light to my path" (NIV). This metaphor extends beyond religious texts, permeating various aspects of our cultural and intellectual heritage.

In ancient Egypt, light was associated with the sun god Ra, who was believed to bring life and order to the world. The Egyptians revered the sun as a source of knowledge and creation, a belief that underscored the importance of enlightenment in their civilization (Assmann, 2001).

Similarly, in Greek mythology, Prometheus is celebrated for bringing fire (a symbol of light and knowledge) to humanity. This act of enlightenment enabled humans to progress and develop civilization, illustrating the transformative power of knowledge (Graves, 1955).

In the Enlightenment period of the 18th century, philosophers like Immanuel Kant emphasized the importance of reason and knowledge as lights that could dispel the darkness of ignorance and superstition. Kant famously defined enlightenment as "man's emergence from his self-imposed immaturity," highlighting the pivotal role of education and critical thinking (Kant, 1784).

In modern times, light continues to symbolize intellectual and spiritual awakening. For instance, UNESCO's International Day of Light celebrates the role light plays in science, culture, and education, reinforcing its enduring significance as a metaphor for knowledge and enlightenment (UNESCO, 2018).

In education, light represents the process of acquiring knowledge and developing critical thinking skills. It embodies the idea of enlightenment—moving from ignorance to understanding. Education shines a light on the world, revealing its complexities and beauty. It empowers individuals to see beyond their immediate experiences and understand broader contexts and perspectives. According to the World Bank, education is a crucial driver of development and poverty reduction, highlighting its role in illuminating pathways to a better future (World Bank, 2018).

Darkness as a Symbol of Ignorance, Prejudice, and Stagnation

Conversely, darkness is often used as a metaphor for ignorance, prejudice, and stagnation. It represents the absence of knowledge and understanding, leading to fear and misconceptions. Ignorance breeds prejudice, causing individuals to judge others based on limited information and preconceived notions. This darkness can manifest in various forms, such as racism, sexism, and other forms of discrimination.

Darkness also symbolizes stagnation—the inability to progress or grow. When people are kept in the dark, they are deprived of opportunities to learn and develop. This can lead to cycles of poverty and social immobility. A report by UNESCO highlights that a lack of education perpetuates poverty, as individuals without access to quality education are more likely to remain in low-income, low-opportunity environments (UNESCO, 2014).

How These Metaphors Will Be Used Throughout the Book to Illustrate Key Points

Throughout "The Path of Light: How Education Defeats

Darkness," the metaphors of light and darkness will be central to illustrating the transformative power of education. Each chapter will explore different facets of this transformation:

1. **Education as Light**: We will delve into how education illuminates minds, broadening perspectives and fostering critical thinking. Stories of students who have experienced this enlightenment will be shared to highlight the real-life impact of learning.
2. **Wisdom and Service**: The book will demonstrate how true wisdom involves not only acquiring knowledge but also applying it to serve others. Examples of service-learning projects and their profound effects on communities will be discussed.
3. **Faith and Spiritual Growth**: By integrating faith with education, we will explore how spiritual enlightenment can enhance intellectual growth. Testimonies of individuals who have found purpose through faith and learning will underscore this connection.
4. **Overcoming Ignorance and Prejudice**: Education's role in combating ignorance and prejudice will be examined, with stories of individuals and communities who have broken free from these chains through learning and understanding.
5. **Addressing Poverty and Addiction**: We will address how education can be a powerful tool in overcoming societal challenges such as poverty and addiction, supported by research and success stories.
6. **Fostering Entrepreneurship**: The book will highlight how education can inspire entrepreneurial thinking, leading to innovation and economic development.

By using these metaphors consistently, the book aims to provide a compelling narrative that underscores the vital importance of education in dispelling the darkness of ignorance and prejudice. Readers will be guided through a journey that not only enlightens their minds but also inspires them to contribute to a brighter, more compassionate world.

I

The Transformative Power of Education

Historical Context: How Education Has Changed Societies

THE ANCIENT WORLD

> *Early Education Systems in Ancient Civilizations*

Education has been a cornerstone of societal development since the dawn of civilization. In ancient Mesopotamia, the cradle of civilization, education was primarily designed to train scribes and administrators. The earliest schools, known as *edubbas*, were established to teach writing and accounting, essential skills for managing the complex bureaucracy of Sumerian city-states (Van De Mieroop, 1999).

In ancient Egypt, education was similarly vital for the

administration. Schools were attached to temples, where students learned to read and write hieroglyphs, essential for maintaining religious and governmental records. Education in Egypt was closely linked to the state's religious and political needs, ensuring the continuity of cultural and administrative traditions (Robins, 1993).

China's ancient education system also played a significant role in shaping its society. The Confucian tradition, which emphasized moral integrity and social harmony, became the foundation of Chinese education. The Imperial Examination system, established during the Han Dynasty, provided a meritocratic route for individuals to enter the bureaucratic elite, significantly influencing social mobility and governance (Elman, 2000).

In ancient Greece, education was seen as a means to cultivate virtuous citizens. The Greeks introduced a more holistic approach to education, incorporating physical, intellectual, and moral training. Institutions like Plato's Academy and Aristotle's Lyceum were not just centers of learning but also forums for philosophical debate and inquiry, profoundly impacting Western thought and education (Jaeger, 1943).

The Role of Education in Shaping Early Societies and Governance

Education in these ancient civilizations was not just about imparting knowledge but also about shaping the social and political structures. In Mesopotamia, the ability to read and write was crucial for maintaining the administrative machinery of the state. The training of scribes ensured the continuity of government and facilitated the management of economic resources (Oppenheim, 1964).

In Egypt, the education of priests and scribes was essential for the functioning of both the religious and administrative systems. The centralized education system helped maintain a cohesive and stable society, with a strong emphasis on cultural and religious continuity (Baines & Yoffee, 1998).

China's Imperial Examination system played a pivotal role in creating a bureaucratic class that was both knowledgeable and loyal to the state. This system helped unify the vast Chinese empire under a common cultural and ideological framework, contributing to its long-term stability and governance (Miyazaki, 1976).

In Greece, education was fundamental to the development of democratic principles. The emphasis on rhetoric, philosophy, and critical thinking in Greek education fostered a culture of debate and civic participation. The educated citizenry of Athens, for instance, played a crucial role in the functioning of its democratic institutions (Ober, 1989).

Examples of Influential Ancient Educators and Philosophers

Several educators and philosophers from ancient civilizations have left a lasting legacy on education and society. Socrates, one of the most renowned Greek philosophers, emphasized the importance of questioning and critical thinking. His method of dialogue and inquiry laid the groundwork for the development of Western philosophical thought and educational practices (Brickhouse & Smith, 1994).

Confucius, the great Chinese philosopher, advocated for an education system that cultivated moral virtues and social harmony. His teachings on ethics, family values, and governance became the cornerstone of Chinese education and had a profound impact on East Asian societies (Yao, 2000).

In addition to these figures, many others, such as Plato, Aristotle, and Egyptian scribes, contributed significantly to the development of educational systems and philosophies that have shaped civilizations throughout history.

The Enlightenment and Beyond

The Impact of the Enlightenment on Modern Education

The Enlightenment, a period spanning the late 17th and 18th centuries, was marked by an intellectual and cultural movement that emphasized reason, individualism, and skepticism of traditional authority. This era profoundly impacted modern education by promoting the idea that knowledge and learning could drive progress and improve human society. Enlightenment thinkers believed that education should be accessible to all and that it was a vital tool for personal and societal transformation (Gay, 1964).

One of the key contributions of the Enlightenment to education was the emphasis on critical thinking and empirical evidence. Philosophers argued that education should not merely transmit knowledge but also cultivate the ability to think independently and question established beliefs. This shift laid the groundwork for modern educational practices that prioritize inquiry-based learning and the scientific method.

Key Figures and Their Contributions to Educational Philosophy

Several Enlightenment figures played crucial roles in shaping educational philosophy. John Locke, an English philosopher, is often regarded as one of the most influential Enlightenment thinkers in education. In his work *Some Thoughts Concerning Education* (1693), Locke advocated for an education that focused on developing reason and virtue. He emphasized the importance of a practical education that prepared individuals for active participation in society (Axtell, 1968).

Jean-Jacques Rousseau, another prominent Enlightenment philosopher, made significant contributions through his work *Emile, or On Education* (1762). Rousseau argued for an education that was natural and child-centered, stressing the importance of allowing children to develop according to their own abilities and interests. He believed that education should nurture the innate goodness of individuals and promote moral and civic virtues (Boyd, 1956).

Immanuel Kant, a German philosopher, also contributed to educational thought by emphasizing the importance of autonomy and moral development. In his essay *What is Enlightenment?* (1784), Kant described enlightenment as "man's emergence from his self-imposed immaturity" and highlighted the role of education in fostering independence and critical thinking (Kant, 1784).

Sir Francis Bacon, an English philosopher and statesman, also significantly influenced educational thought. Bacon is often credited with developing the scientific method, a systematic approach to inquiry that emphasizes observation, experimentation, and empirical evidence. In his work *Novum Organum* (1620), Bacon argued that knowledge should be acquired through inductive reasoning and empirical investigation. His ideas laid the foundation for modern scientific education and encouraged a spirit of inquiry and skepticism that remains central to educational practice today (Vickers, 1992).

The Rise of Public Education and Its Role in Social Progress

The Enlightenment's emphasis on reason and individual rights laid the foundation for the development of public education systems. The idea that education should be a public good accessible to all, regardless of social status, began to take hold. This shift was instrumental in the establishment of compulsory education laws and the expansion of educational opportunities.

In the 19th century, many countries began to implement public education systems. For example, in the United States, Horace Mann, often called the "Father of American Public Education," championed the cause of free, universal education. He believed that public education was essential for creating an informed citizenry and promoting social harmony. Mann's efforts led to the establishment of common schools, which aimed to provide a standardized education for all children (Cremin, 1957).

In Europe, similar movements were underway. In Prussia, the introduction of compulsory education in the early 19th century served as a model for other countries. The Prussian system emphasized rigorous training for teachers and a structured curriculum, contributing to the development of an efficient and effective public education system (Fraser, 2014).

Public education played a crucial role in social progress by reducing inequality and promoting social mobility. By providing access to education for all children, public schools helped break down class barriers and created opportunities for individuals to improve their socioeconomic status. Education became a powerful tool for social change, enabling individuals to participate fully in civic life and contribute to the development of democratic societies.

The 20th and 21st Centuries

Education's Role in Social Movements and Societal Change

Throughout the 20th and 21st centuries, education has been a crucial catalyst for social movements and societal change. During the Civil Rights Movement in the United States, education was both a battleground and a tool for achieving equality. The landmark Supreme Court case Brown v. Board of Education (1954) declared state laws establishing separate public schools for black and white students to be unconstitutional. This decision was pivotal in dismantling racial segregation in schools, setting the stage for broader civil rights advancements (Kluger, 1975).

Education also played a significant role in the women's rights movement. Access to education empowered women to challenge traditional gender roles and seek greater opportunities in professional and public life. The expansion of higher education opportunities for women in the 20th century, supported by legislation such as Title IX of the Education Amendments of 1972, which prohibits gender discrimination in federally funded education programs, was instrumental in promoting gender equality (Ware, 1981).

In recent decades, movements for LGBTQ+ rights, disability rights, and other social justice causes have also leveraged education as a means of advocacy and change. Educational institutions have increasingly become spaces for dialogue, activism, and the promotion of inclusivity, reflecting and driving societal shifts towards greater equality and justice.

Technological Advancements and Their Impact on Education

The advent of technology has revolutionized education in the

20th and 21st centuries. The introduction of computers, the internet, and digital learning tools has transformed how education is delivered and accessed. In the latter half of the 20th century, computers began to be integrated into classrooms, enhancing teaching and learning processes through computer-assisted instruction (CAI) (Molnar, 1997).

The rise of the internet in the 1990s and early 2000s further expanded educational opportunities, enabling the development of online learning platforms and resources. Massive Open Online Courses (MOOCs), launched in the early 21st century, have made high-quality education accessible to millions of learners worldwide, breaking down geographical and financial barriers (Pappano, 2012).

Technological advancements have also facilitated personalized learning, allowing educators to tailor instruction to individual student needs and learning styles. Artificial intelligence (AI) and data analytics are increasingly being used to provide real-time feedback, track student progress, and identify areas for improvement (Luckin et al., 2016).

Globalization and the Shift Towards Inclusive and Equitable Education

Globalization has had a profound impact on education, driving a shift towards more inclusive and equitable educational practices. The increased interconnectedness of the world has highlighted the need for education systems to prepare students for a globalized economy and society. This has led to the incorporation of global perspectives and multicultural education into curricula, promoting cultural awareness and competence (Banks, 2008).

International organizations such as UNESCO and UNICEF have played pivotal roles in advocating for education as a fundamental human right and promoting policies aimed at achieving inclusive and equitable education for all. The United Nations' Sustainable Development Goal 4 (SDG 4) seeks to "ensure inclusive and equitable quality education and promote lifelong learning opportunities for all" by 2030 (UNESCO, 2015).

Efforts to address educational disparities have included initiatives to expand access to education for marginalized and underserved populations, improve educational quality, and eliminate gender disparities. Programs such as the Global Partnership for Education (GPE) have mobilized resources and support to strengthen education systems in developing countries, contributing to significant progress in enrollment and completion rates (GPE, 2018).

Personal Experiences and Examples from AA STEAM & Entrepreneurship Academy

THE FOUNDING VISION

> The Inception of AA STEAM & Entrepreneurship Academy

The AA STEAM & Entrepreneurship Academy is born out of a vision to create an educational environment that not only prepares students for academic and professional success but also instills in them the values of creativity, innovation, and service. Recognizing the limitations of traditional educational models, the Academy is designed to integrate STEAM (Science, Technology, Engineering, Arts, and Mathematics) education with entrepreneurship, creating a holistic learning experience tailored to each student's passions and talents.

The Vision and Mission of the Academy

Our mission at AA STEAM & Entrepreneurship Academy is to provide an educational environment that prepares students for a future of excellence in college, career, and creating new career paths. By integrating STEAMpreneurship and tailoring learning to each student's passions and talents, we aim to cultivate creative thinkers, problem solvers, and career innovators prepared to meet the challenges of tomorrow with confidence.

Our vision for AA STEAM & Entrepreneurship Academy is to pioneer equitable education that nurtures creative minds to innovate and shape the future. We aim to empower our students to become leaders who will forge new career paths, contributing to a world where imagination and entrepreneurship flourish.

Initial Challenges and Triumphs in Establishing the School

Establishing AA STEAM & Entrepreneurship Academy is not without its challenges. From securing funding and facilities to developing a comprehensive curriculum that blends STEAM education with entrepreneurial training, the journey is arduous. However, these challenges are met with determination and innovation, leading to significant triumphs. The academy's success in its early years is a testament to the dedication of its founders, educators, and community supporters.

Innovative Teaching Methods

Description of the STEAM (Science, Technology, Engineering, Arts, and Mathematics) Approach

The AA STEAM & Entrepreneurship Academy employs a STEAM approach to education, emphasizing the interconnectedness of these disciplines. This approach fosters a learning environment where students can explore and integrate knowledge across multiple fields, preparing them for the complexities of the modern world. By incorporating the arts into STEM education, we enhance creativity and innovation, essential skills for the 21st century.

Integration of Entrepreneurship into the Curriculum

One of the unique aspects of our academy is the integration of entrepreneurship into the curriculum. We believe that fostering an entrepreneurial mindset is crucial for preparing students to navigate and succeed in an ever-changing global economy. Our curriculum includes courses and projects that encourage students to develop business ideas, understand market dynamics, and cultivate the skills needed to bring their innovations to life.

Examples of Unique Teaching Methods and Their Impact on Student Engagement and Learning

At AA STEAM & Entrepreneurship Academy, we employ various innovative teaching methods to engage students and enhance learning outcomes. Project-based learning, for instance, allows students to work on real-world problems and develop practical solutions. Collaborative learning environments foster teamwork and communication skills, while personalized learning plans ensure that each student's unique needs and interests are addressed.

Core Values of AA STEAM & Entrepreneurship Academy

- **Innovation and Creativity**: We value creativity and encourage innovative thinking to solve problems and create new opportunities.
- **Individualized Learning**: We believe in tailoring education to each student's passions and talents, recognizing the unique potential in every learner.
- **Excellence and Achievement**: We strive for excellence in all our endeavors, preparing students to achieve their highest potential in college, careers, and entrepreneurship.
- **Equity and Inclusion**: We are committed to providing an equitable education that is inclusive of all students, ensuring every student has the opportunity to succeed.
- **Leadership and Responsibility**: We foster leadership skills in our students, encouraging them to take responsibility for their learning and their impact on the world.
- **Entrepreneurial Mindset**: We promote an entrepreneurial spirit, encouraging students to be proactive, resilient, and innovative in their pursuits.
- **Collaboration and Community**: We value collaboration, fostering a sense of community among students, teachers, parents, and the wider society to support collective growth and success.
- **Integrity and Respect**: We uphold integrity and respect in all our actions, cultivating a culture of honesty, fairness, and mutual respect.

The Need for AA STEAM & Entrepreneurship Academy

In today's rapidly changing world, traditional education systems often fall short of preparing students for the complexities and opportunities of the future. The integration of STEAM education with entrepreneurship at AA STEAM & Entrepreneurship Academy addresses this gap by equipping students with both the technical skills and the innovative mindset needed to thrive.

Moreover, the emphasis on serving others is not only a timeless religious concept but also a crucial component of a well-rounded education. As noted by religious and educational scholars, serving others cultivates empathy, fosters community, and promotes social cohesion (Noddings, 2002). The Bible underscores the importance of service in numerous passages, such as Galatians 5:13, which states, "Serve one another humbly in love" (NIV). By instilling these values, our academy aims to produce graduates who are not only successful but also socially responsible and committed to making the world a better place.

Case Studies of Individuals Transformed Through Education

> # Historical Figures

NELSON MANDELA

Nelson Mandela, one of the most revered figures in modern history, exemplifies the transformative power of education. Born in 1918 in the rural village of Mvezo, South Africa, Mandela's early education was heavily influenced by his African heritage and the oppressive conditions of apartheid. Despite the systemic barriers imposed by the apartheid regime, Mandela pursued education with unwavering determination.

Mandela attended the University of Fort Hare, the only residential university for black students in South Africa at the time. Although he was expelled for participating in a student protest, his educational journey did not end there. He continued his studies via correspondence through the University of South Africa (UNISA), earning a law degree. Mandela's legal education equipped him with the tools to challenge the injustices of apartheid and advocate for human rights and equality (Mandela, 1994).

Throughout his life, Mandela emphasized the importance of education as a means to empower individuals and transform societies. He famously stated, "Education is the most powerful weapon which you can use to change the world." His leadership in the anti-apartheid movement and his presidency in post-apartheid South Africa were profoundly shaped by his educational experiences, highlighting how education can fuel personal and societal change (Mandela, 2003).

MALALA YOUSAFZAI

Malala Yousafzai, born in 1997 in the Swat Valley of Pakistan, is another powerful example of how education can transform lives and societies. Growing up under the Taliban's oppressive regime, which banned girls from attending school, Malala's advocacy for girls' education began at a young age. Her father, an educator and activist, instilled in her the belief that education was a fundamental right for all children.

Malala's outspoken advocacy for education led to a violent attack by the Taliban in 2012 when she was just 15 years old. Despite being critically injured, Malala's resolve only strengthened. She continued her education in the United Kingdom and became a global advocate for girls' education. In 2014, at the age of 17, she became the youngest-ever recipient of the Nobel Peace Prize, recognized for her courage and dedication to the cause of education (Yousafzai, 2013).

Malala's story underscores the transformative power of education, not only in her personal life but also in the global fight for educational equity. Her activism has inspired millions and brought international attention to the barriers faced by girls seeking education in conflict-affected regions (Yousafzai & McCormick, 2014).

> ## Analysis of How Education Played a Pivotal Role in Their Lives and Achievements

NELSON MANDELA

Education was a cornerstone of Nelson Mandela's development as a leader and activist. His legal education provided him with the knowledge and skills to navigate the complexities of the apartheid legal system and mount effective challenges against it. Mandela's time at the University of Fort Hare and UNISA also exposed him to diverse ideas and philosophies, shaping his vision for a democratic and inclusive South Africa. His ability to articulate the injustices of apartheid and propose legal and political reforms was rooted in his educational background (Mandela, 1994).

Mandela's belief in the power of education extended beyond his personal experiences. As President of South Africa, he prioritized education as a means to redress the inequalities of apartheid and build a more equitable society. His efforts to improve access to education for all South Africans have had a lasting impact on the country's educational landscape and continue to inspire educational reforms globally (Mandela, 2003).

MALALA YOUSAFZAI

For Malala Yousafzai, education was both a personal passion and a political statement. Her pursuit of education in defiance of the Taliban's edicts demonstrated the transformative power of knowledge and the importance of standing up for one's rights. Education provided Malala with a platform to amplify her voice and advocate for millions of girls denied the right to learn.

Malala's experiences highlight the role of education in fostering resilience and empowerment. Her ability to recover from the traumatic attack and continue her advocacy is a testament to her belief in the transformative potential of education. By continuing her own education and using her platform to campaign for global educational access, Malala has become a symbol of hope and change, proving that education can indeed transform lives and societies (Yousafzai, 2013).

Stories of Modern-Day Individuals Who Have Overcome Adversity Through Education

OPRAH WINFREY

Oprah Winfrey's life story is a compelling testament to the transformative power of education. Born into poverty in rural Mississippi and facing numerous hardships, including abuse and a troubled home environment, Oprah's early life was marked by adversity. However, education became her pathway to a better future. Despite her difficult circumstances, Oprah excelled in school, earning a scholarship to Tennessee State University, where she studied communication. Her academic success opened doors to opportunities in media, leading to her becoming one of the most influential and successful media personalities in the world (Kelley, 2010).

Oprah's commitment to education extends beyond her personal achievements. She has established educational initiatives such as the Oprah Winfrey Leadership Academy for Girls in South Africa, providing high-quality education to disadvantaged girls and empowering them to overcome their circumstances. Her story highlights how education can be a powerful tool for overcoming adversity and achieving greatness (Oprah Winfrey Leadership Academy Foundation, 2021).

FREEMAN HRABOWSKI

Freeman Hrabowski, the president of the University of Maryland, Baltimore County (UMBC), is another inspiring example. Growing up in the segregated South, Hrabowski was determined to pursue education despite racial barriers. He participated in the Children's Crusade, a pivotal civil rights protest, and went on to excel academically, earning his Ph.D. in higher education administration and statistics. As president of UMBC, Hrabowski has transformed the university into a leading institution for producing African American graduates in STEM fields. His leadership demonstrates the transformative impact of education on individuals and institutions alike (Hrabowski, 2012).

The Role of Education in Breaking Cycles of Poverty and Creating Opportunities

Education is widely recognized as a key factor in breaking the cycles of poverty and creating opportunities for upward mobility. Studies have shown that higher levels of education are associated with increased earnings, improved health outcomes, and greater social mobility (UNESCO, 2014). Education provides individuals with the skills and knowledge needed to access better job opportunities, thereby reducing poverty and improving their quality of life.

EXAMPLE: THE HARLEM CHILDREN'S ZONE

The Harlem Children's Zone (HCZ) is an exemplary initiative that illustrates how education can break the cycle of poverty. Founded by Geoffrey Canada, HCZ provides comprehensive educational and social services to children and families in Harlem, New York. The program includes early childhood education, after-school programs, college preparation, and community support services. Research has shown that HCZ has significantly improved educational outcomes for its participants, leading to higher graduation rates and college attendance (Dobbie & Fryer, 2011).

> ## EXAMPLES OF ENTREPRENEURS AND INNOVATORS WHO ATTRIBUTE THEIR SUCCESS TO THEIR EDUCATIONAL EXPERIENCES

ELON MUSK

Elon Musk, the founder of Tesla and SpaceX, attributes much of his success to his educational background. Musk studied physics and economics at the University of Pennsylvania, which provided him with a strong foundation in problem-solving and analytical thinking. His educational experiences have been instrumental in his ability to innovate and disrupt multiple industries. Musk's success underscores the importance of a solid educational foundation in fostering entrepreneurial thinking and innovation (Vance, 2015).

SARA BLAKELY

Sara Blakely, the founder of Spanx, is another entrepreneur who credits her success to her education. Although she faced numerous rejections early in her career, Blakely's perseverance and educational background in communication helped her develop and market her revolutionary product. Blakely's story highlights how education can equip individuals with the skills and resilience needed to succeed in business (Blakely, 2019).

SUNDAR PICHAI

Sundar Pichai, the CEO of Google and Alphabet Inc., has a remarkable educational background that played a crucial role in his career. Pichai earned his degree in metallurgical engineering from the Indian Institute of Technology Kharagpur, followed by an M.S. in material sciences and engineering from Stanford University, and an MBA from the Wharton School of the University of Pennsylvania. His education provided him with the technical expertise and business acumen required to lead one of the world's largest tech companies. Pichai's success story illustrates the profound impact of a strong educational foundation on career advancement and leadership (Isaacson, 2021).

Impactful Programs and Initiatives

Overview of Educational Programs and Initiatives That Have Transformed Communities

TEACH FOR AMERICA

Teach For America (TFA) is a national organization that recruits and trains college graduates to teach in under-resourced schools across the United States. Founded in 1990, TFA aims to address educational inequality by placing talented teachers in high-need areas. The program has been instrumental in transforming educational outcomes for students in low-income communities. Research indicates that TFA teachers can significantly improve student achievement, particularly in math and science (Kopp, 2011).

KIPP (KNOWLEDGE IS POWER PROGRAM)

The Knowledge Is Power Program (KIPP) is a network of public charter schools that focuses on preparing students from underserved communities for success in college and life. Founded in 1994, KIPP schools emphasize high expectations, rigorous academics, and character development. Studies have shown that KIPP students outperform their peers in traditional public schools, with higher rates of high school graduation and college enrollment (Angrist et al., 2013).

Success Stories from Various Educational Reforms and Interventions

---

FINLAND'S EDUCATION SYSTEM

Finland's education system is widely regarded as one of the best in the world. Finnish schools emphasize equal opportunities, student well-being, and high-quality teacher training. The country's focus on equity and personalized learning has led to outstanding educational outcomes, with Finnish students consistently ranking at the top of international assessments such as PISA (Programme for International Student Assessment). Finland's success demonstrates the importance of investing in teachers and creating an inclusive educational environment (Sahlberg, 2011).

THE SUCCESS FOR ALL (SFA) PROGRAM

The Success for All (SFA) program is a comprehensive school reform model designed to ensure that every child achieves reading proficiency by the third grade. Developed by Robert Slavin and his colleagues at Johns Hopkins University, SFA incorporates cooperative learning, data-driven instruction, and extensive professional development for teachers. Evaluations of SFA have shown significant improvements in reading achievement, particularly for students in high-poverty schools (Slavin et al., 2009).

ROOM TO READ

Room to Read is an international nonprofit organization that focuses on improving literacy and gender equality in education in low-income countries. Since its founding in 2000, Room to Read has established thousands of libraries, published local-language children's books, and supported girls' education programs. The organization's efforts have led to significant increases in literacy rates and educational attainment among the children they serve (Room to Read, 2019).

> ### The Broader Societal Impact of These Programs and Their Potential for Replication

Educational programs and initiatives like Teach For America, KIPP, the Harlem Children's Zone, Finland's education system, the Success for All program, and Room to Read have demonstrated that targeted interventions can lead to substantial improvements in educational outcomes and broader societal benefits. These programs share several common elements: a focus on equity, high expectations, comprehensive support for students and teachers, and data-driven practices.

The success of these initiatives underscores the potential for replicating their models in other contexts. For example, the holistic approach of the Harlem Children's Zone has inspired similar initiatives in other cities, such as the Promise Neighborhoods program in the United States. Similarly, Finland's emphasis on teacher quality and student well-being can serve as a model for other countries seeking to reform their education systems (Tough, 2008).

By learning from these successful programs and adapting their strategies to local contexts, policymakers and educators can work towards creating more equitable and effective education systems worldwide. The broader societal impact of these programs includes increased social mobility, reduced inequality, and the development of a more informed and engaged citizenry.

2

The Universal Call from Darkness to Light: Lessons from World Religions

Knowledge as a Path to Light

Across various religions, the pursuit of knowledge is seen as a means to achieve enlightenment and dispel ignorance. Whether through the study of sacred texts, meditation, or self-reflection, the acquisition of knowledge is viewed as a transformative process that leads individuals from darkness to light. This universal theme highlights the importance of education and lifelong learning in achieving personal and spiritual growth (Prothero, 2010).

THE TRANSFORMATIVE POWER OF KNOWLEDGE IN RELIGIONS

HINDUISM

The Concept of Dharma and Service

In Hinduism, the concept of Dharma is central to living a righteous and fulfilling life. Dharma refers to the moral duties and responsibilities that each individual must follow to maintain social and cosmic order. One of the key aspects of Dharma is selfless service, or "Seva," which involves helping others without expecting anything in return. This principle is reflected in the Bhagavad Gita, where Lord Krishna advises Arjuna to perform his duties selflessly, emphasizing that true knowledge and enlightenment come from serving others and fulfilling one's responsibilities (Bhagavad Gita, 3:19).

The Pursuit of Knowledge and Enlightenment

Hindu philosophy places a strong emphasis on the pursuit of knowledge and enlightenment. The Upanishads, ancient Hindu scriptures, teach that knowledge (Vidya) is the means to dispel ignorance (Avidya) and attain spiritual liberation (Moksha). This pursuit of knowledge is not just intellectual but also spiritual, involving a deep understanding of the self and the universe. The concept of "Jnana Yoga," or the path of knowledge, encourages individuals to seek wisdom and enlightenment through study, meditation, and self-reflection (Radhakrishnan, 1953).

BUDDHISM

Buddhism places a strong emphasis on the pursuit of enlightenment through knowledge and understanding. The Four Noble Truths and the Eightfold Path serve as a guide to overcome suffering and achieve Nirvana. The Buddha taught that ignorance (Avidya) is one of the root causes of suffering and that knowledge and insight can liberate individuals from this cycle. The Dhammapada, a collection of the Buddha's sayings, states, "Just as a candle cannot burn without fire, men cannot live without a spiritual life" (Dhammapada, 146). This underscores the importance of spiritual knowledge in dispelling the darkness of ignorance and leading to enlightenment (Rahula, 1959).

Compassion and Service to Others

Compassion (Karuna) is a fundamental principle in Buddhism. The practice of "Metta," or loving-kindness, involves extending compassion and kindness to all beings. Buddhists believe that serving others and alleviating their suffering is a path to spiritual growth and enlightenment. This principle is exemplified in the Bodhisattva ideal, where individuals strive to attain enlightenment not just for themselves but for the benefit of all sentient beings (Dalai Lama, 1995).

JUDAISM

The Teachings of the Torah on Knowledge and Service

The Torah provides comprehensive teachings on living a righteous life, emphasizing the importance of knowledge and service. The study of Torah is considered a lifelong pursuit, with the belief that it leads to wisdom and understanding. Jewish teachings also emphasize "Tzedakah" (charity) and "Gemilut Chasadim" (acts of kindness), highlighting the importance of helping others and contributing to the well-being of the community (Telushkin, 1991).

Tikkun Olam: Repairing the World

The concept of Tikkun Olam, which means "repairing the world," is central to Jewish thought. It involves actions that improve society and the world at large, reflecting a commitment to social justice and community service. By engaging in Tikkun Olam, individuals fulfill their moral and ethical obligations, contributing to a better and more just world (Doron, 2005).

CHRISTIANITY

Teachings of Jesus on Light and Service

Christianity teaches that Jesus is the "Light of the World," guiding believers out of darkness and into spiritual enlightenment. His teachings emphasize love, compassion, and service to others. The Parable of the Good Samaritan (Luke 10:25-37) and the act of washing the disciples' feet (John 13:1-17) illustrate the importance of serving others and living a life of humility and compassion (Blomberg, 2012).

The Role of Compassion and Charity

Christianity places a strong emphasis on charity (Caritas) and compassion. Believers are encouraged to love their neighbors as themselves and to care for the less fortunate. The concept of "Agape," or selfless love, is central to Christian ethics, promoting acts of kindness and service as a means to live a life reflective of Jesus' teachings (McGrath, 2006).

ISLAM

The Quran's Emphasis on Knowledge and Service

In Islam, the pursuit of knowledge is highly valued. The Quran encourages believers to seek knowledge and wisdom, emphasizing that understanding and education are pathways to greater faith and righteous living. The Hadith, sayings of the Prophet Muhammad, also stress the importance of learning and education (Sahih Muslim, Book 12, Hadith 4005).

Zakat and Social Responsibility

Zakat, one of the Five Pillars of Islam, is a form of almsgiving and social welfare. It requires Muslims to give a portion of their wealth to those in need, promoting social equity and compassion. This practice reflects the broader Islamic principle of social responsibility and the duty to help others, which are integral to a righteous and fulfilling life (Esposito, 2002).

Comparative Analysis of Religious Teachings on Enlightenment and Service

COMMON THEMES OF ENLIGHTENMENT

Moral and Ethical Living

Religious teachings often emphasize moral and ethical living as essential components of enlightenment. Adherents are encouraged to live virtuous lives, guided by principles such as honesty, compassion, and justice. These moral teachings provide a foundation for ethical behavior and social responsibility, promoting harmony and well-being in society (Armstrong, 1993).

SERVICE TO HUMANITY

Helping the Less Fortunate

A common thread among world religions is the call to help the less fortunate. Acts of charity and service are seen as expressions of faith and compassion, fulfilling a moral obligation to support those in need. This principle encourages individuals to engage in selfless acts of kindness, contributing to the overall betterment of society (Kassam, 2010).

COMMUNITY AND SOCIAL WELFARE

Religions often stress the importance of community and social welfare, advocating for actions that benefit the collective good. This emphasis on community service promotes social cohesion and mutual support, reinforcing the idea that individuals have a responsibility to contribute to the well-being of their communities (Patel, 2012).

Practical Applications in Education

INTEGRATING RELIGIOUS TEACHINGS INTO MODERN EDUCATION

Moral and Ethical Education

Incorporating the moral and ethical teachings of various religions into modern education can help students develop a strong sense of integrity and social responsibility. By learning about the values and principles that guide ethical behavior, students can cultivate a deeper understanding of their own beliefs and those of others, fostering mutual respect and empathy (Noddings, 2003).

Community Service Programs

Educational institutions can promote service learning by integrating community service projects into their curricula. These programs provide students with opportunities to apply their knowledge and skills in real-world settings, helping them develop a sense of social responsibility and commitment to community welfare. By engaging in service learning, students can experience firsthand the transformative power of helping others (Eyler & Giles, 1999).

Creating a Holistic Educational Environment

Fostering Empathy and Compassion

Educators can create a compassionate and inclusive learning environment by emphasizing the importance of empathy and understanding. Teaching students to recognize and respect the diverse needs and perspectives of others can help build a supportive and caring community within the classroom and beyond (Miller, 2000).

Encouraging Lifelong Learning and Wisdom

By promoting the pursuit of knowledge and wisdom, educators can inspire students to become lifelong learners. Encouraging critical thinking, reflection, and a love of learning can help students navigate complex challenges and make informed decisions throughout their lives. This approach aligns with the teachings of many religions, which emphasize the continuous search for truth and understanding (Sternberg, 2001).

The Role of Education in Dispelling Darkness

Education is universally recognized as a powerful tool for social and personal transformation. By imparting knowledge, education helps individuals understand the world around them, make informed decisions, and contribute positively to society. This aligns with the religious teachings that view knowledge as a path to enlightenment and moral development.

Moral and Ethical Development

Education fosters moral and ethical development by teaching individuals to distinguish right from wrong, understand the consequences of their actions, and develop a sense of social responsibility. This is reflected in the teachings of many religions, which emphasize the importance of ethical living. For instance, the concept of Dharma in Hinduism, the Eightfold Path in Buddhism, the ethical teachings of the Torah in Judaism, the Sermon on the Mount in Christianity, and the principles of justice in Islam all highlight the role of knowledge in guiding ethical behavior (Armstrong, 1993).

Lifelong Learning and Personal Growth

The pursuit of knowledge is a lifelong endeavor that contributes to personal growth and continuous self-improvement. Religious teachings often stress the importance of lifelong learning as a means to achieve spiritual maturity and enlightenment. For example, the Jewish tradition of Torah study, the Buddhist practice of meditation and learning, and the Islamic emphasis on seeking knowledge all encourage continuous education and reflection (Prothero, 2010).

Creating a Better World

The ultimate goal of education, as reflected in religious teachings, is to create a better world. By dispelling ignorance and fostering understanding, education helps individuals develop the skills and knowledge needed to address societal challenges and contribute to the common good. This aligns with the concept of Tikkun Olam in Judaism, the emphasis on social justice in Christianity, and the principle of Zakat in Islam, all of which highlight the responsibility to improve society through knowledge and action (Doron, 2005).

The pursuit of knowledge is a universal theme across major world religions, emphasizing its role in dispelling darkness and leading to enlightenment. This principle aligns with the modern educational goals of fostering moral and ethical development, promoting lifelong learning, and contributing to the betterment of society. By integrating these religious teachings into educational practices, we can create a more enlightened and compassionate world, fulfilling our collective responsibility to leave the world better than we found it.

3

Jesus, The Great Teacher

Exploration of Jesus' Teachings and His Role as an Educator

JESUS' PEDAGOGICAL APPROACH

Jesus was known for his unique teaching methods, which were highly effective in engaging diverse audiences. One of his primary methods was the use of parables—simple, memorable stories that conveyed profound moral and spiritual lessons. These parables were accessible to people from all walks of life and encouraged listeners to reflect deeply on the messages being conveyed (Blomberg, 2012).

For example, the Parable of the Good Samaritan (Luke 10:25-37) teaches the importance of compassion and neighborly love, transcending cultural and ethnic boundaries. By using relatable scenarios, Jesus made complex ethical concepts understandable and applicable to everyday life.

Jesus also demonstrated a remarkable ability to engage with

various audiences, from scholars and religious leaders to common people and outcasts. He asked probing questions, listened attentively, and tailored his messages to the needs and understanding of his listeners. This inclusive and adaptive approach is a hallmark of effective teaching, emphasizing the importance of knowing and connecting with one's audience (McGrath, 2006).

Jesus' Teaching as a Light to Wake People from Darkness

Jesus' teachings often served as a light to awaken people from darkness, a metaphor for ignorance, prejudice, and moral blindness. By using parables and direct engagement, Jesus illuminated the minds of his listeners, encouraging them to question their assumptions, reflect on their actions, and embrace a higher moral standard. This approach can be tied directly to modern education, where the goal is to enlighten students, promote critical thinking, and encourage ethical behavior.

For instance, the Parable of the Lost Sheep (Luke 15:3-7) highlights the value of every individual and the importance of compassion and forgiveness. Such teachings inspire individuals to recognize the worth of others and act with kindness and empathy, values that are essential in today's diverse and interconnected world. In education, these principles translate into fostering an inclusive environment where every student is valued and supported.

Tying Jesus' Teachings to Education and Entrepreneurship

Removing the religious context, Jesus' teachings can be seen as foundational principles for solving societal problems and fostering an entrepreneurial spirit. Jesus often encouraged his followers to serve others, meet the needs of their communities, and strive for social justice. These are the same qualities that drive successful entrepreneurs and innovators today.

Entrepreneurship in education involves teaching students to identify problems, think creatively, and develop solutions that benefit society. This aligns with Jesus' approach of addressing the immediate needs of his audience and offering practical guidance. For example, when Jesus fed the 5,000 (Matthew 14:13-21), he not only provided a solution to an immediate problem but also demonstrated the importance of resourcefulness and compassion—key traits for any entrepreneur.

Furthermore, Jesus' emphasis on service aligns with the modern concept of social entrepreneurship, where the goal is to create social value rather than just profit. Social entrepreneurs are driven by a mission to make a positive impact on society, reflecting Jesus' teachings on serving others and making a difference in the world.

Inspiring Critical Thinking and Ethical Reflection

Jesus' method of teaching through questions and dialogue encouraged his listeners to think critically and reflect on their own beliefs and behaviors. This Socratic method is a powerful educational tool that promotes deep understanding and personal growth. In modern education, fostering critical thinking skills is essential for preparing students to navigate complex problems and make informed decisions.

For example, in the Parable of the Prodigal Son (Luke 15:11-32), Jesus invites listeners to reflect on themes of forgiveness, redemption, and unconditional love. This parable challenges individuals to reconsider their judgments and embrace a more compassionate and understanding perspective. Similarly, education should challenge students to question their assumptions, consider multiple perspectives, and develop a well-rounded, ethical worldview.

Jesus' teachings, whether viewed through a religious or secular lens, offer valuable insights for modern education. His use of parables to convey complex moral lessons, his ability to engage diverse audiences, and his emphasis on compassion, service, and critical thinking are all principles that can enhance educational practices today. By integrating these timeless values into the curriculum, educators can help students become enlightened individuals who are capable of solving problems, serving their communities, and making a positive impact on the world.

Parallels Between Jesus' Teachings and Modern Educational Philosophies

STUDENT-CENTERED LEARNING

Jesus' teaching methods align closely with the principles of student-centered learning, which prioritize the needs, interests, and abilities of each student. By using parables and direct engagement, Jesus ensured that his teachings were relevant and meaningful to his audience. Modern educational philosophies similarly emphasize the importance of personalized learning experiences that cater to individual student needs. John Dewey, a prominent educational reformer, advocated for experiential education where learning is rooted in the interests and experiences of students. Dewey believed that education should be an interactive and dynamic process, reflecting Jesus' approach of engaging directly with his audience and addressing their specific contexts (Dewey, 1938).

HOLISTIC EDUCATION

Holistic education seeks to develop the whole person—intellectually, emotionally, socially, and spiritually. Jesus' teachings addressed not only moral and spiritual issues but also practical aspects of living a virtuous life. This comprehensive approach to education encourages the integration of character education and social-emotional learning into the curriculum, fostering well-rounded individuals. Jack Miller, a leading advocate for holistic education, emphasizes that true education should nurture the mind, body, and spirit, reflecting the interconnectedness of all aspects of human development. This aligns with Jesus' teachings, which encompassed ethical behavior, personal integrity, and social responsibility (Miller, 2000).

COLLABORATIVE LEARNING

Jesus often taught in group settings, encouraging dialogue and interaction among his followers. This collaborative approach mirrors modern educational practices that promote teamwork, communication, and the sharing of diverse perspectives. Building a sense of community and fostering collaborative learning environments can enhance student engagement and deepen understanding. Research by David and Roger Johnson highlights the effectiveness of cooperative learning, where students work together to achieve common goals, enhancing both academic achievement and interpersonal skills (Johnson & Johnson, 1989).

SERVANT LEADERSHIP IN EDUCATION

Jesus exemplified servant leadership, a concept that emphasizes leading by serving others. In education, this translates to teachers and administrators who prioritize the well-being and development of their students. By modeling humility, empathy, and selflessness, educators can inspire students to adopt similar values and become leaders who serve their communities. Robert Greenleaf, who coined the term "servant leadership," argued that the best leaders are those who serve others and prioritize the growth and well-being of their communities. This philosophy is integral to creating educational environments that foster leadership and civic responsibility (Greenleaf, 1977).

KNOWLEDGE AS LIGHT: BRIDGING ANCIENT WISDOM AND MODERN EDUCATION

Knowledge has long been equated with light, symbolizing enlightenment, clarity, and understanding. This metaphor is prevalent in many cultural and religious traditions, including Christianity, where Jesus is often referred to as the "Light of the World" (John 8:12). This metaphor can be effectively applied to modern educational philosophies, which view knowledge as a tool for dispelling ignorance and fostering personal and societal growth.

In modern educational contexts, the acquisition of knowledge is seen as a pathway to empowerment and social change. Paulo Freire, a Brazilian educator and philosopher, argued that education is a practice of freedom, enabling individuals to perceive and address the injustices in their lives. Freire's concept of "conscientization" involves developing a critical awareness of one's social reality through reflection and action, mirroring Jesus' approach of enlightening his followers and encouraging them to think critically about their lives and actions (Freire, 1970).

INTEGRATING JESUS' TEACHINGS INTO MODERN EDUCATIONAL PRACTICES

By drawing parallels between Jesus' teachings and contemporary educational philosophies, we can create a more holistic and inclusive approach to education. This involves:

1. **Personalized Learning**: Tailoring educational experiences to meet the unique needs and interests of each student, much like Jesus addressed the individual concerns of his listeners.
2. **Holistic Development**: Fostering intellectual, emotional, social, and spiritual growth, ensuring that students develop into well-rounded individuals.
3. **Collaborative Learning**: Promoting teamwork and community building, encouraging students to learn from and with each other.
4. **Servant Leadership**: Instilling values of humility, empathy, and service, preparing students to lead by serving others.

By integrating these principles, educators can create learning environments that not only impart knowledge but also inspire students to become compassionate, thoughtful, and proactive members of society.

Lessons from the Life of Jesus on Service, Compassion, and Wisdom

THE ROLE OF SERVICE IN EDUCATION

Jesus taught by serving others, as illustrated in the act of washing his disciples' feet (John 13:1-17). This lesson highlights the importance of humility and service, which are essential components of a meaningful education. In this act, Jesus demonstrated that true leadership involves serving others, a principle that can transform educational environments. Encouraging students to engage in community service projects can instill a sense of social responsibility and compassion, teaching them to look beyond their own needs and contribute positively to society.

Service in education not only benefits the community but also enriches students' learning experiences. It fosters a sense of connection and purpose, helping students develop empathy and a deeper understanding of societal issues. Research has shown that students who participate in community service are more likely to develop a strong sense of civic responsibility and social consciousness (Eyler & Giles, 1999). By incorporating service into the curriculum, educators can help students experience the transformative power of serving others, aligning with Jesus' teachings.

CULTIVATING COMPASSION

Compassionate teaching practices involve understanding and addressing the diverse needs of students. Jesus' interactions with marginalized individuals, such as the healing of the leper (Matthew 8:1-4), demonstrate the importance of empathy and inclusivity. He reached out to those who were often ignored or ostracized by society, offering them healing and acceptance. This approach can be applied in education by fostering a classroom environment that promotes empathy, understanding, and support for all students, regardless of their backgrounds or abilities.

Compassion in education involves creating a supportive and inclusive environment where every student feels valued and respected. Educators can achieve this by practicing active listening, showing empathy, and providing individualized support. Nel Noddings, an educational theorist, emphasizes the importance of caring in education, arguing that relationships built on mutual respect and understanding are essential for effective teaching and learning (Noddings, 2003). By modeling compassion, teachers can inspire students to develop empathy and care for others, mirroring the approach of Jesus.

WISDOM IN EDUCATION

Wisdom involves the application of knowledge and experience to make sound judgments and decisions. Jesus encouraged his followers to seek wisdom and understanding, as seen in his teachings and parables. For example, in the Parable of the Wise and Foolish Builders (Matthew 7:24-27), Jesus illustrated the importance of building one's life on a solid foundation of wisdom and discernment. This principle is highly relevant in education, where fostering wisdom involves encouraging critical thinking, reflection, and a lifelong love of learning.

Wisdom in education goes beyond the mere acquisition of knowledge; it involves teaching students to think critically, analyze information, and make informed decisions. Robert Sternberg, a psychologist and researcher, describes wisdom as the ability to balance personal interests with the common good, making choices that benefit both oneself and society (Sternberg, 2001). By integrating wisdom into the curriculum, educators can help students develop the ability to navigate complex life challenges with insight and discernment.

THE LIGHT OF KNOWLEDGE PULLS YOU FROM DARKNESS

The metaphor of light as knowledge is deeply rooted in many

cultural and religious traditions, including Christianity. In the Bible, Jesus is often referred to as the "Light of the World" (John 8:12), symbolizing the enlightenment and guidance he provides to humanity. This metaphor can be applied to education, where knowledge serves as a beacon, illuminating the path to understanding and personal growth.

Knowledge has the power to dispel ignorance and prejudice, pulling individuals out of the darkness of misunderstanding and into the light of awareness and wisdom. Education enables individuals to see the world more clearly, understand complex issues, and make informed decisions. It promotes critical thinking and encourages individuals to question assumptions, fostering a deeper understanding of themselves and the world around them.

For example, in the Parable of the Lamp (Luke 8:16-18), Jesus teaches that one does not light a lamp and hide it but places it where it can illuminate the entire room. This parable emphasizes the importance of sharing knowledge and enlightenment with others, a principle that is central to education. By spreading knowledge, educators can help students move from darkness to light, empowering them to become informed and engaged members of society.

Jesus' teachings on service, compassion, and wisdom offer valuable lessons for modern education. By incorporating these principles into educational practices, educators can create environments that not only impart knowledge but also inspire students to become compassionate, thoughtful, and proactive individuals. The light of knowledge has the power to transform lives, dispelling the darkness of ignorance and prejudice and guiding students toward a brighter, more enlightened future.

4

Overcoming Ignorance and Prejudice

Defining Ignorance and Prejudice and Their Impact on Society

UNDERSTANDING IGNORANCE

Definition and Nature of Ignorance

Ignorance can be defined as a lack of knowledge or information. It manifests in various forms, including willful ignorance, where individuals choose to remain uninformed, and cultural ignorance, where people are unaware of the customs, beliefs, and practices of other cultures. Willful ignorance involves deliberately avoiding information that might challenge one's beliefs or assumptions, leading to a refusal to acknowledge facts. Cultural ignorance, on the other hand, stems from a lack of exposure to or understanding of different cultural norms and practices (Smithson, 2008).

In religious and philosophical contexts, ignorance is often viewed as a form of darkness, obscuring one's understanding and preventing enlightenment. This metaphorical use of darkness underscores the idea that ignorance impedes growth and development. As Jesus said while he was dying, "Father, forgive them, for they know not what they do" (Luke 23:34, NIV), highlighting the profound impact of ignorance on human behavior and the importance of seeking understanding and forgiveness.

Impact of Ignorance on Individuals and Society

Ignorance perpetuates stereotypes and misinformation, leading to misunderstandings and conflict. Stereotypes are oversimplified and generalized beliefs about a particular group of people, often based on incomplete or inaccurate information. These stereotypes can lead to prejudiced attitudes and discriminatory behaviors, as individuals make assumptions about others without truly understanding them (Nussbaum, 2010).

On a societal level, ignorance can result in poor decision-making, economic stagnation, and social strife. For instance, policymakers who are uninformed about the complexities of a particular issue may implement ineffective or harmful policies. Economic stagnation can occur when ignorance prevents innovation and adaptation to changing circumstances. Social strife, including conflicts between different cultural or ethnic groups, is often fueled by ignorance and misunderstanding (Nussbaum, 2010).

For individuals, ignorance limits opportunities for personal growth and understanding, creating barriers to social mobility and integration. People who lack knowledge and awareness may find it difficult to access education and employment opportunities, perpetuating cycles of poverty and marginalization. Furthermore, ignorance can hinder personal relationships, as individuals struggle to connect with others who have different experiences and perspectives (Nussbaum, 2010).

UNDERSTANDING PREJUDICE

Definition and Nature of Prejudice

Prejudice is a preconceived opinion that is not based on reason or actual experience. It encompasses various forms, including racial, religious, and gender-based prejudices. Prejudice stems from stereotypes, fear, and a lack of understanding, leading to discriminatory attitudes and behaviors (Dovidio et al., 2010).

Racial prejudice involves negative attitudes and beliefs about individuals based on their race or ethnicity. These prejudices are often rooted in historical injustices and perpetuated by societal structures and cultural norms. Religious prejudice involves discrimination against individuals based on their religious beliefs or practices, often resulting from misunderstandings and fear of the unknown. Gender-based prejudice involves biased attitudes and behaviors towards individuals based on their gender, often reinforcing harmful stereotypes and limiting opportunities for women and non-binary individuals (Dovidio et al., 2010).

Prejudice is often fueled by fear and a lack of understanding. When individuals do not have accurate information or direct experiences with people from different backgrounds, they may rely on stereotypes and misinformation to form their opinions. This can lead to a cycle of prejudice and discrimination, as negative attitudes are reinforced by social and cultural norms (Dovidio et al., 2010).

Impact of Prejudice on Individuals and Society

Prejudice fosters discrimination and inequality, marginalizing certain groups and denying them equal opportunities. Discrimination involves unjust or prejudicial treatment of individuals based on their membership in a particular group, and it can occur in various settings, including the workplace, educational institutions, and social interactions. This marginalization can lead to disparities in education, employment, healthcare, and other areas, perpetuating cycles of poverty and social exclusion (Allport, 1954).

Prejudice can cause significant psychological harm, including low self-esteem, anxiety, and depression. Individuals who experience discrimination and prejudice may struggle with feelings of worthlessness and hopelessness, impacting their mental health and overall well-being. This psychological harm can also affect physical health, as chronic stress and anxiety can lead to various health issues (Allport, 1954).

Prejudice creates divisions within society, undermining social cohesion and hindering collective progress. When certain groups are marginalized and discriminated against, it creates an "us vs. them" mentality, leading to social fragmentation and conflict. This lack of unity and cooperation can hinder efforts to address common challenges and achieve shared goals, ultimately weakening the social fabric (Allport, 1954).

In addition to these impacts, prejudice and ignorance can also perpetuate systemic inequalities and injustices. For example, racial prejudice and discrimination can lead to disparities in criminal justice outcomes, with marginalized groups facing harsher penalties and higher rates of incarceration. Similarly, gender-based prejudice can result in unequal pay and limited career advancement opportunities for women, reinforcing economic disparities and limiting social mobility (Allport, 1954).

Ignorance and prejudice are deeply intertwined, with ignorance often serving as the root cause of prejudiced attitudes and behaviors. By understanding the nature and impact of these issues, we can begin to address them through education, dialogue, and inclusive practices. As Jesus' teachings remind us, forgiveness and understanding are crucial in overcoming ignorance and fostering a more compassionate and just society. By promoting knowledge and awareness, we can dispel the darkness of ignorance and create a more equitable and inclusive world.

Educational Strategies to Combat Ignorance and Promote Understanding

CURRICULUM DEVELOPMENT

Inclusive Education

Developing an inclusive curriculum involves incorporating diverse perspectives and histories, which is crucial for combating ignorance and promoting understanding. By presenting a broad range of viewpoints, students gain a more comprehensive understanding of the world and the people in it. This approach helps to challenge existing stereotypes and biases, fostering a more inclusive and empathetic worldview.

Teaching critical thinking and media literacy is essential for empowering students to question and deconstruct biased information. When students are equipped with these skills, they are better able to identify and challenge misinformation and stereotypes. This not only helps to dispel ignorance but also promotes a culture of inquiry and open-mindedness. Research has shown that critical thinking and media literacy education can significantly reduce the acceptance of misinformation and increase the ability to critically evaluate sources (Banks, 2015).

For example, integrating lessons on the civil rights movement, women's suffrage, and indigenous histories into the curriculum can help students understand the struggles and contributions of various groups. This inclusion fosters a sense of shared humanity and encourages students to see beyond their own experiences.

Cultural Competence Education

Cultural competence education promotes understanding and respect for different cultures. Programs that encourage students to explore and appreciate cultural diversity foster a more inclusive and empathetic worldview. Such education is essential for preparing students to thrive in a globalized society, where cross-cultural interactions are increasingly common.

Cultural competence education involves more than just learning about other cultures; it requires an ongoing commitment to understanding and valuing diversity. This can include activities such as cultural exchange programs, multicultural events, and curriculum that includes diverse voices and perspectives. Research has shown that students who receive cultural competence education are more likely to develop positive attitudes towards diversity and exhibit less prejudice (Gay, 2010).

For instance, including literature from diverse authors, history from multiple perspectives, and art from various cultures in the curriculum can help students develop a deeper appreciation for the richness of human experience. This approach not only combats ignorance but also prepares students to navigate and contribute positively to an interconnected world.

Classroom Practices

Dialogues and Discussions

Facilitating open dialogues about prejudice and ignorance in the classroom creates a safe space for students to share their experiences and learn from each other. These discussions help students develop empathy and a deeper understanding of different perspectives. By engaging in meaningful conversations about difficult topics, students can confront their own biases and learn to appreciate the experiences of others.

Research supports the effectiveness of structured dialogues in reducing prejudice and promoting understanding. According to hooks (1994), open and honest conversations about race, gender, and other social issues can lead to greater empathy and reduced prejudice. Teachers play a crucial role in moderating these discussions, ensuring that they are respectful and productive.

In practice, teachers can use techniques such as circle discussions, where each student has an opportunity to speak and listen, and Socratic seminars, which encourage critical thinking and respectful debate. These methods help students articulate their thoughts, listen to others, and engage in constructive dialogue.

Service Learning and Community Engagement

Service learning projects that connect students with diverse communities encourage empathy and social responsibility. By engaging in community service, students can apply their knowledge in real-world contexts, fostering a sense of connection and purpose. Service learning integrates academic learning with meaningful community service, allowing students to address real-world problems while developing a deeper understanding of the issues facing their communities.

Research has shown that service learning can have a profound impact on students' attitudes towards diversity and social responsibility. Eyler and Giles (1999) found that students who participate in service learning projects are more likely to develop a sense of empathy, civic responsibility, and commitment to social justice.

Examples of service learning projects include partnering with local organizations to address issues such as homelessness, environmental sustainability, or educational inequality. These projects provide students with hands-on experience in working with diverse populations and understanding the complexities of social issues.

TEACHER TRAINING

Professional Development

Professional development programs that train teachers to recognize and address their own biases are crucial for creating inclusive and supportive classroom environments. These programs equip teachers with strategies to handle prejudice and promote inclusivity, ensuring that all students feel valued and respected.

Research has shown that teachers' biases can significantly impact student outcomes, particularly for marginalized groups. Professional development focused on cultural competence, anti-bias training, and inclusive teaching practices can help teachers become more aware of their biases and develop strategies to mitigate their impact (Villegas & Lucas, 2002).

Effective professional development includes workshops, seminars, and ongoing training sessions that provide teachers with practical tools and resources. Topics might include understanding implicit bias, developing culturally responsive pedagogy, and implementing inclusive classroom strategies.

Mentorship and Support

Providing ongoing support and mentorship for teachers implementing inclusive practices helps sustain these efforts. Continuous professional development and peer support networks are vital for maintaining an inclusive and effective educational environment.

Mentorship programs pair experienced educators with those who are newer to inclusive practices, providing guidance, feedback, and support. This ongoing mentorship helps teachers navigate challenges and refine their approaches. Additionally, peer support networks allow teachers to share resources, strategies, and experiences, fostering a collaborative and supportive professional community (Cochran-Smith, 2004).

For example, schools can establish professional learning communities (PLCs) where teachers regularly meet to discuss best practices, reflect on their teaching, and plan collaborative projects. These communities of practice are essential for sustaining long-term change and ensuring that inclusive education practices are deeply embedded in the school culture.

Addressing ignorance and prejudice through education requires a comprehensive approach that includes inclusive curriculum development, effective classroom practices, and robust teacher training. By fostering critical thinking, cultural competence, and empathy, educators can create environments where students learn to appreciate diversity and challenge stereotypes. These educational strategies are essential for dispelling the darkness of ignorance and promoting a more just and inclusive society.

Stories of Students Who Have Overcome Prejudice Through Education

CASE STUDIES

Breaking Racial Barriers

Ruby Bridges

Ruby Bridges grew up in the racially segregated South and faced tremendous challenges due to racial prejudice. In 1960, at the age of six, she became the first African American student to integrate an all-white elementary school in the South. Ruby faced intense hostility from white parents and students, requiring federal marshals to escort her to school every day. Despite the adversity, Ruby's courage and determination, supported by her family and teachers, helped break racial barriers in education (Coles, 1995).

Ruby's education journey was marked by isolation; she was

taught alone by her teacher, Barbara Henry, who provided not only academic instruction but also emotional support. This experience highlighted the importance of inclusive education and the role of supportive educators in helping students overcome prejudice. Ruby Bridges' story illustrates how educational opportunities can foster personal growth and contribute to broader social change (Bridges, 1999).

PERSONAL NARRATIVES

Reflective Essays by Students

Michelle Obama

Michelle Obama's memoir, *Becoming*, provides a powerful narrative of overcoming prejudice through education. Growing up on the South Side of Chicago, Michelle faced racial and socioeconomic challenges. Despite these obstacles, her dedication to education led her to Princeton University and Harvard Law School. Michelle's educational experiences, including overcoming stereotypes and proving her capabilities in predominantly white institutions, were transformative (Obama, 2018).

In her reflective essays and speeches, Michelle emphasizes the importance of mentorship and support systems in education. She highlights how her teachers and mentors played critical roles in her academic and personal development, enabling her to navigate and overcome prejudice. Her story serves as an inspiration for students facing similar challenges, illustrating the impact of inclusive and supportive educational environments (Obama, 2018).

INTERVIEWS AND TESTIMONIALS

Ta-Nehisi Coates

In interviews and his book *Between the World and Me*, Ta-Nehisi Coates discusses his experiences with racial prejudice and the role of education in his life. Growing up in Baltimore, Coates faced systemic racism and violence, which profoundly shaped his worldview. Education provided him with a pathway to understand and articulate his experiences, leading him to become a renowned author and journalist (Coates, 2015).

Coates credits his teachers and mentors for encouraging his intellectual curiosity and critical thinking skills. Their support helped him navigate the challenges of racial prejudice and inspired him to pursue higher education. Coates' testimonials highlight the transformative power of education in fostering resilience and understanding, demonstrating the critical role of educators in supporting students from marginalized backgrounds (Coates, 2015).

Overcoming ignorance and prejudice requires a concerted effort from educators, students, and communities. By understanding the nature and impact of ignorance and prejudice, implementing effective educational strategies, and learning from the experiences of those who have overcome these challenges, we can create a more inclusive and understanding society. Education, as a path to enlightenment, empowers individuals to dispel darkness and contribute to a better world. Real-life stories like those of Ruby Bridges, Malala Yousafzai, Michelle Obama, and Ta-Nehisi Coates provide powerful examples of how education can break down barriers and promote social justice.

5

Serving Others: The Heart of True Education

The Importance of Teaching Service and Compassion in Education

THE ROLE OF SERVICE IN PERSONAL DEVELOPMENT

> Developing Empathy and Emotional Intelligence

Service and compassion are foundational elements in developing empathy and emotional intelligence in students. Empathy, the ability to understand and share the feelings of another, is crucial for building meaningful relationships and fostering a sense of community. Emotional intelligence, which encompasses self-awareness, self-regulation, motivation, empathy, and social skills, is equally important for personal and professional success.

Research indicates that engaging in service activities helps students develop a deeper understanding of others' experiences and challenges, enhancing their empathetic abilities. For example, a study by Morelli et al. (2015) found that participating in community service activities increases empathic concern and perspective-taking among students. These experiences allow students to see the world from different viewpoints, fostering a sense of compassion and understanding that transcends their immediate surroundings.

Building Character and Moral Integrity

Service learning also plays a significant role in building character and moral integrity. By participating in service projects, students are exposed to real-world issues that require ethical decision-making and a commitment to social justice. This exposure helps students develop a strong moral compass and a sense of responsibility towards others.

According to Berkowitz and Bier (2005), character education that includes service learning components is effective in promoting ethical behavior and moral reasoning. When students engage in activities that benefit others, they learn the importance of honesty, fairness, and respect. These values become ingrained in their character, guiding their actions and decisions throughout their lives.

EDUCATIONAL BENEFITS OF TEACHING COMPASSION

Enhancing Student Engagement and Motivation

Teaching compassion and service has been shown to enhance student engagement and motivation. When students are involved in meaningful activities that have a positive impact on others, they are more likely to feel a sense of purpose and connection to their learning. This intrinsic motivation can lead to higher levels of academic achievement and a greater commitment to education.

A study by Deci and Ryan (2000) on self-determination theory suggests that activities promoting autonomy, competence, and relatedness—key components of service learning—enhance intrinsic motivation and engagement. When students perceive their efforts as meaningful and see the tangible results of their actions, their motivation to learn and contribute increases significantly.

Promoting a Positive School Culture and Climate

Incorporating service and compassion into the educational framework also promotes a positive school culture and climate. Schools that emphasize these values create an environment where students feel safe, respected, and valued. This positive climate is essential for effective learning and overall student well-being.

Research by Battistich et al. (1997) highlights the connection between a caring school environment and student outcomes. Schools that foster a culture of caring and compassion report lower levels of bullying, higher student morale, and better academic performance. By prioritizing service and compassion, schools can create a supportive community that enhances both social and academic development.

Teaching service and compassion in education is not just about enhancing academic performance; it is about shaping well-rounded, empathetic individuals who are prepared to contribute positively to society. Developing empathy and emotional intelligence, building character and moral integrity, enhancing student engagement and motivation, and promoting a positive school culture are all critical outcomes of integrating service and compassion into the educational experience. As we strive to prepare students for the challenges of the future, these values will guide them in creating a more compassionate and equitable world.

Examples of Service Projects and Their Impact on Students and Communities

SCHOOL-BASED SERVICE PROJECTS

> Organizing Local Community Clean-Up Events

Local community clean-up events are excellent opportunities for students to engage in service while fostering a sense of environmental responsibility. These projects involve students working together to clean parks, streets, and other public areas, promoting a cleaner and more pleasant environment for the community.

Research indicates that participating in community clean-up projects can have a significant impact on students' environmental awareness and civic responsibility. According to a study by Wells and Lekies (2006), children who participate in environmental activities are more likely to develop pro-environmental attitudes and behaviors. These activities help students understand the importance of taking care of their surroundings and the collective effort required to maintain a healthy environment.

Implementing Peer Tutoring and Mentorship Programs

Peer tutoring and mentorship programs are another effective way for students to engage in service. These programs involve older or more advanced students providing academic support and guidance to their peers. This not only helps the mentees improve their academic skills but also enhances the tutors' understanding of the subject matter and their ability to communicate effectively.

Research has shown that peer tutoring programs can lead to significant academic and social benefits for both tutors and tutees. According to Topping (2005), peer tutoring improves academic performance, enhances self-esteem, and fosters a sense of belonging and connection within the school community. These programs also help develop leadership skills and promote a culture of collaboration and mutual support among students.

COMMUNITY PARTNERSHIP PROJECTS

Collaborating with Local Non-Profits for Food Drives and Shelters

Collaborating with local non-profits for food drives and shelters provides students with the opportunity to address pressing social issues such as hunger and homelessness. These projects involve collecting and distributing food and essential items to those in need, as well as volunteering at shelters to provide support and companionship.

Research highlights the positive impact of such projects on students' social awareness and empathy. A study by Youniss and Yates (1997) found that students who participate in community service projects develop a greater understanding of social inequalities and a stronger commitment to civic engagement. These experiences help students recognize their capacity to make a difference and inspire them to continue serving their communities.

Partnering with Senior Centers for Intergenerational Learning Activities

Partnering with senior centers for intergenerational learning activities allows students to engage with older adults, fostering mutual understanding and respect across generations. These activities can include storytelling sessions, technology assistance, arts and crafts, and shared learning experiences.

Research suggests that intergenerational programs provide numerous benefits for both students and seniors. According to Kaplan and Hanhardt (2003), these programs enhance students' communication and social skills, increase their empathy for older adults, and provide valuable life lessons. For seniors, interacting with young people can reduce feelings of isolation, improve cognitive function, and enhance their overall well-being.

School-based service projects and community partnership initiatives offer powerful opportunities for students to engage in meaningful service while developing important life skills. Organizing local community clean-up events and implementing peer tutoring and mentorship programs help students build environmental responsibility, academic skills, and leadership qualities. Collaborating with local non-profits for food drives and shelters and partnering with senior centers for intergenerational learning activities foster social awareness, empathy, and intergenerational understanding. These projects not only benefit students but also create positive, lasting impacts on the communities they serve.

How Service Learning Can Cultivate Empathy and Social Responsibility

INTEGRATING SERVICE LEARNING INTO THE CURRICULUM

> Designing Service Learning Projects That Align with Academic Goals

Integrating service learning into the curriculum involves designing projects that align closely with academic goals, making learning both meaningful and practical. Service learning projects are structured to apply classroom knowledge to real-world issues, thereby enhancing students' understanding and retention of academic content.

For example, a biology class might involve students in a project to create a community garden. This project allows students to apply their knowledge of plant biology, ecosystems, and sustainability while contributing to local food security. In an English class, students might organize a literacy campaign, where they use their skills in writing, communication, and organization to promote reading within the community.

Research indicates that service learning projects aligned with academic goals lead to higher academic achievement and improved critical thinking skills. According to a study by Billig (2000), students engaged in service learning demonstrate greater mastery of content and improved problem-solving abilities. By integrating service learning into the curriculum, educators can create a dynamic and engaging learning environment that fosters both intellectual and social growth.

Reflective Practices to Deepen Learning and Personal Growth

Reflective practices are a crucial component of service learning, helping students to internalize and understand their experiences. Reflection encourages students to think critically about the service activities they participate in, the impact of their work, and the personal and social issues they encounter. This process deepens learning and promotes personal growth by helping students connect their service experiences to broader academic and life goals.

Reflection can take various forms, including journaling, group discussions, presentations, and digital storytelling. For instance, after participating in a community clean-up event, students might write reflective essays on what they learned about environmental stewardship and community engagement. Alternatively, students might engage in group discussions to share their experiences and insights, fostering a deeper understanding of the social issues they addressed.

Research supports the importance of reflection in service learning. Eyler, Giles, and Schmiede (1996) found that structured reflection enhances the learning outcomes of service learning by helping students make connections between their service activities and academic content. Reflective practices also promote empathy and social responsibility by encouraging students to consider the perspectives of those they serve and the broader societal implications of their work.

By incorporating reflective practices into service learning, educators can help students develop critical thinking skills, empathy, and a sense of social responsibility. This process not only enhances academic learning but also fosters personal and civic growth, preparing students to become thoughtful, engaged citizens.

Integrating service learning into the curriculum and incorporating reflective practices are essential strategies for cultivating empathy and social responsibility in students. Designing service learning projects that align with academic goals ensures that students apply classroom knowledge to real-world issues, enhancing their understanding and retention of academic content. Reflective practices deepen learning and promote personal growth by encouraging students to critically examine their experiences and their impact on the community. These strategies create a dynamic and engaging learning environment that prepares students to become compassionate, responsible, and active members of society.

Long-Term Impact of Service Learning

CASE STUDIES OF STUDENTS WHO HAVE BEEN TRANSFORMED BY SERVICE LEARNING

> ### Case Study 1: From Student to Community Leader

Jessica's Journey through City Year

Jessica Posner, co-founder of the non-profit organization Shining Hope for Communities (SHOFCO), exemplifies the transformative power of service learning. During her college years, Jessica participated in City Year, a national service program that places young adults in high-need urban schools. Her service experience in under-resourced communities exposed her to the challenges faced by marginalized populations and ignited her passion for social justice and community development.

Through her service, Jessica developed a deep understanding of the systemic issues contributing to poverty and educational inequities. This hands-on experience was instrumental in shaping her career path. After City Year, Jessica co-founded SHOFCO, an organization dedicated to combating urban poverty and gender inequality in Kenya's slums. Her journey from a service learning participant to a community leader underscores the lasting impact of service learning on personal and professional development (Posner, 2010).

> ### Case Study 2: Bridging Cultural Gaps

Brian's Work with Amigos de las Américas

Brian Stevenson, a former participant in the Amigos de las Américas program, provides another compelling example. Amigos de las Américas is a service learning program that sends young volunteers to Latin American countries to work on community development projects. Brian's experience in a rural community in Nicaragua was life-changing. He worked on projects related to public health and education, collaborating closely with local residents.

Brian's service learning experience deepened his cultural competence and empathy. He learned to navigate cultural differences and build meaningful relationships with people from diverse backgrounds. This experience profoundly influenced his academic and career choices, leading him to study international relations and pursue a career in global health. Brian's journey illustrates how service learning can foster a lifelong commitment to cross-cultural understanding and social justice (Stevenson, 2015).

RESEARCH FINDINGS ON THE LASTING BENEFITS OF SERVICE LEARNING FOR CIVIC ENGAGEMENT

Enhanced Civic Responsibility and Participation

Research consistently shows that service learning has a lasting impact on students' civic responsibility and participation. Astin and Sax (1998) found that students who engage in service learning are more likely to develop a strong sense of civic responsibility and continue participating in community service and civic activities throughout their lives. This increased civic engagement stems from the real-world experiences and reflections that service learning provides, helping students understand the importance of active citizenship and community involvement.

Development of Social and Emotional Skills

Service learning also promotes the development of crucial social and emotional skills, which are essential for civic engagement. These skills include empathy, teamwork, leadership, and problem-solving. Scales, Blyth, Berkas, and Kielsmeier (2000) found that students who participate in service learning programs show significant improvements in these areas, which in turn enhance their ability to contribute effectively to their communities. These skills not only support civic engagement but also prepare students for success in their personal and professional lives.

Long-Term Academic and Career Benefits

In addition to fostering civic engagement, service learning has been linked to long-term academic and career benefits. Markus, Howard, and King (1993) indicate that students who participate in service learning demonstrate higher levels of academic achievement and are more likely to pursue careers in public service and non-profit sectors. The practical experience gained through service learning projects helps students develop a clear sense of purpose and direction, guiding their educational and career choices.

Promotion of Lifelong Learning and Community Involvement

Service learning encourages a mindset of lifelong learning and continuous community involvement. Students who engage in service learning are more likely to seek out additional educational opportunities and remain active in community organizations as adults. This commitment to lifelong learning and community service helps build stronger, more resilient communities (Eyler & Giles, 1999).

The long-term impact of service learning is evident in the transformative experiences of individuals like Jessica Posner and Brian Stevenson, as well as in extensive research findings. Service learning not only enhances civic responsibility and social skills but also provides long-term academic and career benefits. By fostering a mindset of lifelong learning and community involvement, service learning prepares students to become engaged, compassionate, and proactive members of society.

6

Poverty, Addiction, and the Path to Enlightenment

Understanding Poverty and Addiction as Manifestations of Darkness

THE NATURE AND CAUSES OF POVERTY

Economic, Social, and Structural Factors

Poverty is a multifaceted issue deeply rooted in economic, social, and structural factors. Economically, poverty is often driven by unemployment, underemployment, and low wages, which prevent individuals from meeting their basic needs. Economic instability, such as recessions and market downturns, exacerbates these conditions, making it difficult for people to escape the poverty cycle.

Social factors include the lack of access to quality education, healthcare, and social services. Communities with limited resources struggle to provide opportunities for upward mobility, trapping individuals in a cycle of poverty. Discrimination based on race, gender, and ethnicity further limits access to these resources, creating systemic barriers that are difficult to overcome. According to the World Bank, social inequality is a significant predictor of poverty, as marginalized groups often face additional challenges that hinder their economic progress (World Bank, 2020).

Structural factors involve the broader economic and political systems that shape society. Policies that fail to address income inequality, inadequate social safety nets, and insufficient public investment in infrastructure contribute to persistent poverty. For instance, regions with poor transportation and housing infrastructure limit residents' access to jobs and essential services, perpetuating economic hardship.

Psychological Impact of Poverty on Individuals and Communities

The psychological impact of poverty is profound and far-reaching. Living in poverty is associated with chronic stress, which can lead to a host of mental health issues such as anxiety, depression, and substance abuse. The constant struggle to secure basic necessities creates an environment of uncertainty and insecurity, which takes a toll on mental well-being.

Research shows that children growing up in poverty are particularly vulnerable to psychological stress. The American Psychological Association (APA) reports that poverty-related stress can impair cognitive development and academic performance, leading to long-term educational and economic disadvantages (APA, 2019). These children are more likely to experience behavioral problems and have difficulty forming healthy relationships, further compounding their challenges.

Poverty also impacts communities by fostering environments where crime and violence are more prevalent. The lack of economic opportunities can lead to feelings of hopelessness and frustration, which may result in higher crime rates and social unrest. This creates a vicious cycle, where communities struggling with poverty and violence become even more isolated and deprived of the resources needed for recovery and growth.

In summary, poverty is not merely an economic condition but a complex interplay of various factors that deeply affect individuals and communities. Understanding these causes and impacts is crucial for developing effective interventions and policies aimed at alleviating poverty and its associated psychological burdens.

Poverty, as a manifestation of darkness, stems from a confluence of economic, social, and structural factors, and its psychological impacts are both profound and pervasive. Addressing poverty requires a holistic approach that considers these diverse elements and aims to provide comprehensive support and opportunities for individuals and communities. By understanding the intricate nature of poverty, we can work towards creating enlightened solutions that bring individuals out of the darkness of poverty and into the light of opportunity and well-being.

THE NATURE AND CAUSES OF ADDICTION

Biological, Psychological, and Social Contributors to Addiction

Addiction is a complex condition influenced by a combination of biological, psychological, and social factors. Understanding these contributors is crucial for developing effective prevention and treatment strategies.

BIOLOGICAL FACTORS

Biologically, addiction is often linked to genetic predispositions and neurochemical changes in the brain. Research indicates that genetic factors can account for 40-60% of an individual's susceptibility to addiction (NIDA, 2018). Variations in genes affecting neurotransmitter systems, such as dopamine, can influence how individuals experience pleasure and reward, making them more susceptible to addictive behaviors. Chronic substance use alters brain chemistry, leading to changes in brain structure and function that reinforce the cycle of addiction. For example, repeated use of addictive substances can diminish the brain's ability to produce natural dopamine, making it difficult for individuals to experience pleasure without the substance (Koob & Volkow, 2016).

PSYCHOLOGICAL FACTORS

Psychologically, addiction can stem from various factors, including trauma, mental health disorders, and coping mechanisms. Individuals with unresolved trauma or co-occurring mental health conditions, such as depression, anxiety, or PTSD, are more likely to use substances as a form of self-medication. This coping mechanism can quickly lead to dependency and addiction. The stress-relief and temporary escape provided by substances can create a powerful psychological association, making it difficult for individuals to break free from their addictive behaviors (Khantzian, 2017).

SOCIAL FACTORS

Socially, addiction is influenced by environmental factors such as family dynamics, peer pressure, and socioeconomic status. Individuals raised in environments where substance use is prevalent or normalized are at a higher risk of developing addiction. Additionally, peer pressure, especially during adolescence, can play a significant role in initiating substance use. Socioeconomic factors, including poverty, lack of education, and limited access to healthcare, also contribute to the likelihood of addiction. Communities with high levels of unemployment and social instability often see higher rates of substance abuse as individuals seek to escape their challenging circumstances (SAMHSA, 2020).

THE CYCLICAL RELATIONSHIP BETWEEN POVERTY AND ADDICTION

Poverty and addiction are deeply intertwined, creating a vicious cycle that is difficult to break. Poverty increases the risk of addiction, and addiction, in turn, exacerbates poverty, creating a feedback loop that perpetuates both conditions.

POVERTY AS A RISK FACTOR FOR ADDICTION

Living in poverty exposes individuals to a range of stressors, including financial instability, lack of access to basic needs, and social isolation. These stressors can lead individuals to seek solace in substances, which temporarily alleviate their hardships but ultimately contribute to addiction. Additionally, impoverished areas often lack access to quality education and employment opportunities, limiting individuals' prospects for upward mobility. The absence of these opportunities can lead to feelings of hopelessness and desperation, driving individuals towards substance use as a coping mechanism (Galea & Vlahov, 2002).

ADDICTION PERPETUATING POVERTY

Once addiction takes hold, it exacerbates the conditions of poverty. Individuals struggling with addiction may face difficulties maintaining employment, managing finances, and fulfilling familial responsibilities. This can lead to job loss, financial ruin, and strained relationships, further entrenching individuals in poverty. The costs associated with sustaining an addiction can deplete financial resources, leaving individuals and their families in dire economic straits. Moreover, addiction can lead to legal issues and health complications, both of which incur additional costs and hinder an individual's ability to escape poverty (NIDA, 2020).

BREAKING THE CYCLE

Addressing the cyclical relationship between poverty and addiction requires comprehensive interventions that target both conditions simultaneously. Effective strategies include providing access to quality addiction treatment services, enhancing economic opportunities through education and job training programs, and offering social support services to address the underlying causes of both poverty and addiction. By tackling these issues holistically, it is possible to break the cycle and help individuals achieve lasting recovery and improved quality of life.

Understanding the biological, psychological, and social contributors to addiction, as well as the cyclical relationship between poverty and addiction, is essential for developing effective interventions. By addressing these intertwined issues, we can create pathways to recovery and stability, helping individuals move from the darkness of addiction and poverty to the light of health and prosperity.

Educational Approaches to Addressing These Issues

INTEGRATING LIFE SKILLS AND FINANCIAL LITERACY

> Teaching Essential Life Skills for Self-Sufficiency

Integrating life skills education into the curriculum is crucial for helping individuals overcome the challenges associated with poverty and addiction. Life skills encompass a range of abilities, including critical thinking, decision-making, problem-solving, and effective communication. These skills are essential for self-sufficiency and resilience, enabling individuals to navigate life's complexities and make informed decisions.

Programs that focus on teaching life skills have been shown to significantly improve outcomes for individuals at risk of poverty and addiction. For example, the World Health Organization (WHO) emphasizes that life skills education enhances personal and social development, which is vital for mental health and well-being (WHO, 1997). By equipping students with these skills, educational institutions can help them build a strong foundation for future success.

FINANCIAL LITERACY PROGRAMS TO BREAK THE CYCLE OF POVERTY

Financial literacy is another critical component of education that can help break the cycle of poverty. Understanding financial concepts such as budgeting, saving, investing, and managing credit is essential for economic stability and growth. Financial literacy programs empower individuals to make sound financial decisions, avoid debt, and build wealth over time.

Research indicates that financial literacy education has a positive impact on financial behaviors and outcomes. A study by Lusardi and Mitchell (2014) found that individuals with higher financial literacy are more likely to plan for retirement, save regularly, and manage their finances effectively. By incorporating financial literacy into the curriculum, educators can provide students with the tools they need to achieve financial independence and security.

TEACHING ESSENTIAL LIFE SKILLS FOR SELF-SUFFICIENCY

Critical Thinking and Problem-Solving

Critical thinking and problem-solving are essential life skills that enable individuals to analyze situations, consider alternatives, and make informed decisions. These skills are particularly important for those facing the challenges of poverty and addiction, as they must navigate complex social and economic environments.

Educational programs that emphasize critical thinking and problem-solving can help students develop these abilities. For instance, project-based learning (PBL) and inquiry-based learning (IBL) are effective methods for fostering these skills. According to a study by Bell (2010), PBL and IBL engage students in meaningful, real-world problems, enhancing their critical thinking and problem-solving capabilities. These approaches encourage students to take ownership of their learning, collaborate with peers, and apply their knowledge to practical situations.

EFFECTIVE COMMUNICATION AND INTERPERSONAL SKILLS

Effective communication and interpersonal skills are vital for building relationships, accessing resources, and advocating for oneself. These skills are particularly important for individuals recovering from addiction or striving to overcome poverty, as they often need to interact with social services, healthcare providers, and potential employers.

Programs that focus on developing communication and interpersonal skills can significantly improve individuals' ability to navigate social systems and build supportive networks. Role-playing, group discussions, and collaborative projects are effective strategies for teaching these skills. Research by Durlak et al. (2011) found that social and emotional learning (SEL) programs, which include communication and interpersonal skills training, lead to improved social behaviors, academic performance, and emotional well-being.

FINANCIAL LITERACY PROGRAMS TO BREAK THE CYCLE OF POVERTY

> Budgeting and Saving

Understanding how to create and manage a budget is a fundamental aspect of financial literacy. Budgeting allows individuals to track their income and expenses, set financial goals, and allocate resources effectively. Teaching students how to budget can help them develop healthy financial habits that prevent overspending and promote saving.

Programs that incorporate practical budgeting exercises and real-life scenarios can make financial literacy education engaging and relevant. For example, the "Money Matters" program by Junior Achievement teaches students how to create a budget, manage expenses, and understand the importance of saving. According to a study by Mandell and Klein (2009), students who participate in such programs demonstrate improved financial knowledge and behaviors, including increased savings and more prudent spending.

INVESTING AND MANAGING CREDIT

In addition to budgeting and saving, understanding investing and credit management is crucial for long-term financial health. Educating students about the principles of investing, such as risk and return, diversification, and compound interest, can help them build wealth and achieve financial goals. Similarly, teaching about credit management, including how to use credit responsibly and the impact of credit scores, can prevent debt and financial instability.

Financial literacy programs that include interactive tools and simulations can enhance students' understanding of these concepts. For instance, the "Stock Market Game" allows students to experience investing in a simulated environment, helping them learn about market dynamics and investment strategies. Research by Walstad, Rebeck, and MacDonald (2010) shows that students who participate in such programs have a better grasp of financial concepts and are more likely to engage in positive financial behaviors.

Integrating life skills and financial literacy into educational curricula is essential for addressing the challenges of poverty and addiction. Teaching essential life skills such as critical thinking, problem-solving, and effective communication empowers individuals to navigate complex environments and make informed decisions. Financial literacy programs provide the knowledge and tools necessary for economic stability and growth, helping individuals break the cycle of poverty. By equipping students with these skills, educational institutions can foster resilience, self-sufficiency, and long-term success.

Providing Supportive and Inclusive Educational Environments

CREATING TRAUMA-INFORMED AND SUPPORTIVE LEARNING SPACES

Creating trauma-informed and supportive learning environments is essential for helping students affected by poverty and addiction. Trauma-informed education acknowledges the impact of adverse experiences on students' ability to learn and provides a framework for creating safe, supportive spaces where all students can thrive.

UNDERSTANDING TRAUMA-INFORMED EDUCATION

Trauma-informed education involves understanding the widespread impact of trauma and recognizing the signs and symptoms in students. This approach emphasizes safety, trustworthiness, peer support, collaboration, empowerment, and cultural sensitivity. Educators trained in trauma-informed practices can better support students who have experienced trauma, fostering resilience and academic success.

Research underscores the importance of trauma-informed approaches in education. A study by Dorado et al. (2016) found that implementing trauma-informed practices in schools led to significant improvements in student behavior, attendance, and academic performance. By creating an environment that prioritizes emotional and physical safety, schools can help mitigate the adverse effects of trauma and promote a positive learning experience.

Strategies for Creating Supportive Learning Spaces

Several strategies can be employed to create trauma-informed and supportive learning environments:

1. **Professional Development for Educators**: Training teachers and staff on trauma-informed practices is crucial. This includes understanding trauma's effects, recognizing symptoms, and implementing supportive strategies in the classroom. Professional development programs can equip educators with the knowledge and skills needed to support traumatized students effectively.
2. **Positive Behavioral Interventions and Supports (PBIS)**: PBIS is a proactive approach that promotes positive behavior through reinforcement and support rather than punishment. Implementing PBIS can create a more inclusive and supportive school climate, reducing disciplinary issues and improving student outcomes (Sugai & Horner, 2002).
3. **Social-Emotional Learning (SEL) Programs**: SEL programs

teach students essential skills for managing emotions, building relationships, and making responsible decisions. Research by Durlak et al. (2011) shows that SEL programs improve students' social skills, behavior, and academic performance. Integrating SEL into the curriculum can help students develop resilience and coping strategies.

IMPLEMENTING PROGRAMS FOR MENTAL HEALTH AND ADDICTION RECOVERY

Addressing mental health and addiction issues within the educational environment is critical for supporting students affected by these challenges. Schools can play a vital role in providing resources and programs that promote mental well-being and facilitate recovery.

SCHOOL-BASED MENTAL HEALTH SERVICES

Providing access to mental health services within schools can significantly impact students' well-being. School-based mental health programs offer counseling, therapy, and support for students dealing with various issues, including anxiety, depression, and trauma. These services can help students manage their mental health, improving their ability to focus and succeed academically.

Research highlights the effectiveness of school-based mental health services. A study by Greenberg et al. (2003) found that students who received mental health support in schools showed significant improvements in behavior, emotional regulation, and academic achievement. By integrating mental health services into the educational setting, schools can provide timely and accessible support for students in need.

PROGRAMS FOR ADDICTION RECOVERY

Implementing programs specifically designed for addiction recovery is also essential. These programs can provide education about substance abuse, offer counseling and support groups, and connect students with community resources for recovery.

One effective approach is the use of school-based health centers (SBHCs), which provide comprehensive health services, including addiction treatment and recovery support. SBHCs have been shown to improve health outcomes and reduce substance abuse among students. A study by Guo et al. (2008) found that students who accessed SBHC services reported lower rates of substance use and improved overall health.

PEER SUPPORT AND MENTORSHIP PROGRAMS

Peer support and mentorship programs can also play a vital role in supporting students with mental health and addiction issues. These programs pair students with trained peers or mentors who provide guidance, support, and encouragement. Peer support can reduce stigma, increase engagement in recovery, and improve mental health outcomes.

Research by Larkin et al. (2016) indicates that peer mentorship programs for substance use recovery lead to higher rates of sustained recovery and improved psychosocial outcomes. By fostering a supportive community, schools can help students navigate the challenges of addiction and mental health recovery.

Providing supportive and inclusive educational environments is crucial for addressing the needs of students affected by poverty and addiction. Creating trauma-informed learning spaces and implementing mental health and addiction recovery programs can significantly improve students' well-being and academic success.

By prioritizing safety, support, and inclusivity, educators can help students overcome the challenges they face and achieve their full potential.

Success Stories of Individuals Overcoming These Challenges Through Education

CASE STUDIES OF INDIVIDUALS OVERCOMING POVERTY

> Profiles of Individuals Who Used Education to Escape Poverty

Dr. Ben Carson

Dr. Ben Carson's journey from poverty to becoming a world-renowned neurosurgeon is a testament to the transformative power of education. Growing up in a single-parent household in inner-city Detroit, Carson faced significant economic and social challenges. His mother, who had only a third-grade education, encouraged her sons to read and learn, despite their financial struggles.

Carson's academic journey began to change when he developed a love for reading. This newfound passion helped him improve his grades and gain confidence in his abilities. He went on to attend Yale University, where he studied psychology, and later, the University of Michigan Medical School, where he pursued a degree in neurosurgery. His dedication to education enabled him to overcome the barriers of poverty and achieve extraordinary success in his field (Carson, 1992).

Sonia Sotomayor

Sonia Sotomayor, the first Hispanic and third woman to serve on the U.S. Supreme Court, also rose from humble beginnings through the power of education. Raised in a public housing project in the Bronx, Sotomayor faced numerous challenges, including financial hardship and her father's early death. Her mother emphasized the importance of education and hard work as the means to a better life.

Sotomayor excelled academically, earning a scholarship to Princeton University and later attending Yale Law School. Her educational achievements opened doors to prestigious legal positions and eventually led to her appointment to the Supreme Court. Sotomayor's story illustrates how education can serve as a powerful equalizer, enabling individuals from disadvantaged backgrounds to reach the highest levels of success (Sotomayor, 2013).

ANALYSIS OF THE EDUCATIONAL PROGRAMS THAT SUPPORTED THEIR SUCCESS

Head Start Program

One of the key educational programs that has helped individuals like Carson and Sotomayor succeed is the Head Start program. Established in 1965, Head Start provides early childhood education, health, nutrition, and parent involvement services to low-income children and families. Research has shown that participants in the Head Start program are more likely to graduate from high school, attend college, and achieve higher earnings compared to their peers who did not participate (Garces, Thomas, & Currie, 2002).

Upward Bound

Upward Bound, a federally funded program, has also played a crucial role in helping low-income students prepare for and succeed in higher education. The program offers academic support, college counseling, and enrichment activities to high school students from disadvantaged backgrounds. Studies have demonstrated that Upward Bound participants are more likely to enroll in and graduate from college than non-participants (Myers & Schirm, 1999).

Mentorship and Scholarship Programs

Mentorship and scholarship programs have been instrumental in supporting individuals like Carson and Sotomayor. These programs provide financial assistance, academic guidance, and emotional support to students from low-income families. For example, the Gates Millennium Scholars Program, funded by the Bill & Melinda Gates Foundation, has helped thousands of minority students achieve their educational goals by providing scholarships and support services. Research indicates that recipients of such programs have higher retention and graduation rates compared to their peers (Fenske, Geranios, Keller, & Moore, 2000).

The success stories of individuals like Dr. Ben Carson and Justice Sonia Sotomayor highlight the transformative power of education in overcoming poverty. Educational programs such as Head Start, Upward Bound, and various mentorship and scholarship initiatives have played a critical role in supporting these individuals on their paths to success. By providing access to quality education and support services, these programs help break the cycle of poverty and enable individuals to achieve their full potential.

Case Studies of Individuals Overcoming Addiction

STORIES OF RECOVERY AND EDUCATIONAL REHABILITATION

Russell Brand

Russell Brand, a well-known comedian, actor, and author,

struggled with addiction for many years before achieving recovery and transforming his life through education and rehabilitation. Brand's journey to sobriety was marked by numerous relapses and challenges, but his commitment to recovery and personal growth was unwavering. He credits much of his success to the structured support and educational programs he engaged in during his rehabilitation.

Brand participated in various 12-step programs, which provided a framework for understanding his addiction and developing strategies for long-term recovery. These programs emphasized the importance of self-awareness, accountability, and continuous learning. Brand has since become an advocate for addiction recovery and mental health awareness, using his platform to educate others about the complexities of addiction and the pathways to recovery (Brand, 2017).

David Sheff and Nic Sheff

David Sheff, a journalist, and his son Nic Sheff, an author, provide a compelling case study of addiction and recovery through their respective memoirs, *Beautiful Boy* and *Tweak*. Nic struggled with severe addiction to methamphetamines and other substances, leading to multiple stints in rehab and several relapses. His journey to recovery was long and arduous, but education played a pivotal role in his rehabilitation.

Nic found that writing and reflecting on his experiences were therapeutic and instrumental in his recovery process. Educational rehabilitation programs that incorporated creative expression and therapeutic writing helped Nic to process his trauma and develop coping mechanisms. His father's persistent efforts to understand addiction and support his son's recovery through education and research were also crucial. David Sheff's book highlights the importance of family education and involvement in the recovery process (Sheff, 2008; Sheff, 2009).

THE ROLE OF SUPPORTIVE EDUCATIONAL ENVIRONMENTS IN ADDICTION RECOVERY

Creating Safe and Supportive Spaces

Supportive educational environments play a critical role in the recovery process for individuals overcoming addiction. These environments provide a safe space where individuals can learn, grow, and heal without judgment or stigma. Key elements of supportive educational environments include:

1. **Non-Judgmental Atmosphere**: Creating a non-judgmental atmosphere is crucial for individuals in recovery. This involves training educators and staff to understand addiction as a medical condition rather than a moral failing. Research by Luoma et al. (2007) shows that reducing stigma associated with addiction improves treatment outcomes and encourages individuals to seek help.
2. **Holistic Support Services**: Providing holistic support services, such as counseling, peer support groups, and wellness programs, helps address the multifaceted nature of addiction. Educational institutions that offer comprehensive support services create an environment where individuals can address their physical, emotional, and psychological needs. A study by Harris et al. (2008) found that integrated support services significantly enhance recovery outcomes.

Implementing Educational Rehabilitation Programs

Educational rehabilitation programs are designed to support

individuals in their recovery journey by providing structured learning opportunities and life skills training. These programs often include:

1. **Life Skills Training**: Programs that teach essential life skills, such as stress management, communication, and financial literacy, help individuals build a foundation for a stable and healthy life. Life skills training empowers individuals to handle everyday challenges without resorting to substance use. Research by Botvin and Griffin (2004) indicates that life skills training is effective in preventing substance abuse and promoting long-term recovery.
2. **Vocational and Educational Training**: Providing vocational and educational training helps individuals in recovery gain new skills and improve their employability. These programs offer pathways to meaningful employment, which is a critical factor in sustaining recovery. Studies show that individuals who engage in vocational training are more likely to achieve and maintain sobriety (Laudet et al., 2007).

PEER SUPPORT AND MENTORSHIP

Peer support and mentorship are vital components of supportive educational environments. Connecting individuals in recovery with peers who have successfully navigated similar challenges provides encouragement and practical guidance. Mentorship programs facilitate the sharing of experiences and coping strategies, fostering a sense of community and belonging.

Research by Tracy and Wallace (2016) highlights the positive impact of peer support on addiction recovery. Individuals who participate in peer support programs report higher levels of motivation, increased self-efficacy, and greater resilience. By integrating peer support into educational settings, institutions can enhance the recovery process and support long-term success.

The stories of individuals like Russell Brand and Nic Sheff demonstrate the transformative power of supportive educational environments in overcoming addiction. Creating safe and non-judgmental spaces, implementing educational rehabilitation programs, and fostering peer support are essential strategies for supporting individuals in their recovery journey. By providing comprehensive and compassionate support, educational institutions can play a crucial role in helping individuals overcome addiction and achieve lasting recovery.

7

Entrepreneurship as a Path to Light

The Role of Entrepreneurship in Creating Opportunities and Combating Poverty

ECONOMIC EMPOWERMENT THROUGH ENTREPRENEURSHIP

Generating Income and Employment Opportunities

Entrepreneurship plays a pivotal role in generating income and creating employment opportunities, particularly in communities grappling with poverty. By establishing new businesses, entrepreneurs can drive economic activity, which in turn creates jobs and stimulates local economies. This process not only provides direct employment but also fosters a multiplier effect, where the creation of one job can lead to additional employment opportunities as the demand for goods and services increases.

A study by the Global Entrepreneurship Monitor (GEM) found that entrepreneurial activity is a significant driver of job creation, particularly in developing countries. The GEM 2020/2021 Global Report indicates that in economies where entrepreneurship is thriving, there is a notable reduction in unemployment rates and an increase in economic stability (Bosma et al., 2021). This demonstrates that supporting entrepreneurship can be a strategic approach to combating poverty by providing sustainable livelihoods and economic security.

Entrepreneurship also allows individuals to leverage their unique skills and talents, often creating niche markets that were previously underserved. This ability to innovate and fill gaps in the market not only generates income for the entrepreneurs themselves but also meets the needs of their communities, fostering a more resilient and diverse economy.

PROMOTING ECONOMIC GROWTH AND DEVELOPMENT

Beyond job creation, entrepreneurship is a catalyst for broader economic growth and development. Entrepreneurs drive innovation, bringing new products and services to market, which can increase productivity and efficiency across various industries. This innovation is critical for economic development as it often leads to the creation of entirely new sectors and industries, contributing to a diversified and robust economy.

Entrepreneurship contributes significantly to gross domestic product (GDP) growth. A report by the Organization for Economic Co-operation and Development (OECD) highlights that small and medium-sized enterprises (SMEs), many of which are entrepreneurial ventures, account for a substantial share of GDP in both developed and developing countries (OECD, 2017). By driving innovation and competition, these businesses help economies to expand and evolve, ensuring long-term economic sustainability.

Moreover, entrepreneurship can play a transformative role in addressing economic disparities. By providing opportunities for marginalized groups, including women, minorities, and low-income individuals, entrepreneurship promotes inclusive growth. Programs that support underrepresented entrepreneurs have been shown to reduce income inequality and foster a more equitable distribution of wealth. For instance, initiatives like microfinance and social entrepreneurship have empowered millions of people worldwide, enabling them to start their own businesses and lift themselves out of poverty.

Grameen Bank

A compelling example of entrepreneurship promoting economic empowerment is the Grameen Bank in Bangladesh, founded by Nobel Laureate Muhammad Yunus. Grameen Bank provides microloans to impoverished individuals, primarily women, who lack access to traditional banking services. These microloans enable recipients to start small businesses, generate income, and achieve financial independence.

Research has shown that the Grameen Bank model has significantly improved the economic conditions of its borrowers. A study by Khandker and Samad (2014) found that microcredit programs like Grameen Bank's have led to increased household income, higher levels of employment, and greater economic stability in rural Bangladesh. This model has been replicated in various forms around the world, demonstrating the powerful impact of entrepreneurship on poverty reduction and economic development.

Entrepreneurship is a vital force for generating income, creating employment opportunities, and promoting economic growth and development. By fostering innovation and providing pathways out of poverty, entrepreneurial activities contribute significantly to economic empowerment and social progress. Supporting entrepreneurship, particularly in underserved communities, can lead to sustainable economic development and a more equitable distribution of wealth, ultimately contributing to the overall well-being of society.

SOCIAL IMPACT OF ENTREPRENEURSHIP

> Addressing Social Issues and Improving Community Well-Being

Entrepreneurship goes beyond economic benefits; it also plays a crucial role in addressing social issues and enhancing community well-being. Social entrepreneurs, in particular, focus on creating businesses that solve societal problems, ranging from healthcare and education to environmental sustainability and social justice. By addressing these issues through innovative solutions, entrepreneurs can significantly improve the quality of life in their communities.

One notable example is the work of TOMS Shoes, founded by Blake Mycoskie. TOMS Shoes operates on a one-for-one business model, where for every pair of shoes sold, another pair is donated to a child in need. This initiative has provided millions of shoes to children in impoverished regions, improving their health and access to education. Studies have shown that proper footwear can prevent soil-transmitted infections and enhance school attendance by protecting children's feet from injuries and infections (Blake et al., 2020).

Social entrepreneurship often focuses on creating sustainable solutions that empower communities. For instance, companies like Warby Parker, which donates glasses to those in need for every pair sold, address vision impairment in underserved communities. Clear vision is critical for education and employment, and providing affordable eyewear has a direct impact on individuals' ability to learn and work effectively.

ENCOURAGING INNOVATION AND PROBLEM-SOLVING IN UNDERSERVED AREAS

Entrepreneurs are inherently problem solvers who use innovation to address challenges, particularly in underserved areas. These regions often face unique problems, such as inadequate infrastructure, limited access to education and healthcare, and high unemployment rates. Entrepreneurs who focus on these areas can introduce innovative solutions that not only address these challenges but also foster long-term development.

For example, in many parts of Africa, access to reliable electricity is a significant issue. M-KOPA Solar, a Kenyan company, addresses this problem by providing affordable solar-powered devices to off-grid households. Customers pay for the solar devices through a mobile payment system, making it accessible even to low-income families. This innovation has not only provided clean energy to millions of households but also created job opportunities and stimulated economic activity in the region (Gates, 2018).

Another impactful example is the work of Sanergy, a social enterprise based in Kenya that addresses the issue of inadequate sanitation in urban slums. Sanergy builds low-cost, high-quality sanitation facilities and franchises them to local entrepreneurs, who maintain the facilities and charge a small fee for usage. The waste collected is then converted into valuable end-products like organic fertilizer and renewable energy. This model addresses public health issues, creates jobs, and promotes environmental sustainability (Sanergy, 2017).

EMPOWERING MARGINALIZED GROUPS

Entrepreneurship also has the power to empower marginalized groups by providing them with the tools and resources needed to improve their circumstances. Women, minorities, and individuals from low-income backgrounds often face significant barriers to economic participation. Social entrepreneurship can help overcome these barriers by offering targeted support and opportunities.

Programs like Kiva, a non-profit organization that allows people to lend money to low-income entrepreneurs via the internet, have enabled many individuals to start or expand their businesses. By providing microloans to entrepreneurs in over 80 countries, Kiva helps to create economic opportunities for people who are typically excluded from traditional financial systems. Research has shown that microfinance initiatives like Kiva can lead to increased economic activity and improved quality of life for recipients (Morduch, 1999).

Entrepreneurship significantly contributes to social impact by addressing pressing social issues, fostering innovation, and improving community well-being. Through initiatives like TOMS Shoes, Warby Parker, M-KOPA Solar, and Sanergy, entrepreneurs demonstrate how innovative solutions can solve societal problems and empower communities. By encouraging entrepreneurship in underserved areas and supporting marginalized groups, we can create sustainable change and promote a more equitable and prosperous society.

How Education Can Foster Entrepreneurial Mindsets

INTEGRATING ENTREPRENEURSHIP EDUCATION INTO THE CURRICULUM

> Teaching Business Fundamentals and Financial Literacy

Integrating entrepreneurship education into the curriculum is essential for fostering an entrepreneurial mindset among students. Teaching business fundamentals, such as understanding markets, developing business plans, and managing finances, equips students with the knowledge and skills needed to start and sustain their own ventures.

A solid foundation in financial literacy is particularly crucial. Students who understand financial concepts such as budgeting, saving, investing, and credit management are better prepared to make informed decisions that affect their personal and business finances. According to the National Financial Educators Council, financial literacy empowers individuals to achieve their financial goals and enhances economic stability (NFEC, 2020).

Programs like Junior Achievement (JA) offer comprehensive curricula that cover business fundamentals and financial literacy. JA programs have been shown to improve students' business acumen and financial understanding significantly. A study by De Haan et al. (2012) found that students who participated in JA programs demonstrated a better understanding of business concepts and financial management, as well as increased entrepreneurial intentions.

ENCOURAGING CREATIVITY AND INNOVATION THROUGH PROJECT-BASED LEARNING

Project-based learning (PBL) is an effective method for encouraging creativity and innovation, which are critical components of entrepreneurship. PBL involves students working on real-world projects that require them to apply their knowledge and skills to solve complex problems. This hands-on approach not only enhances learning but also fosters the development of critical thinking, collaboration, and problem-solving abilities.

In the context of entrepreneurship education, PBL can involve students in activities such as developing business plans, creating marketing strategies, and launching mock startups. These projects provide students with practical experience and the opportunity to experiment with innovative ideas in a supportive environment.

Research supports the effectiveness of PBL in fostering an entrepreneurial mindset. A study by Boaler (1999) found that students engaged in PBL demonstrated higher levels of engagement, creativity, and problem-solving skills compared to those in traditional learning environments. Furthermore, students involved in PBL were more likely to take initiative and think critically about the challenges they faced, key traits of successful entrepreneurs.

CASE EXAMPLE: STANFORD D.SCHOOL

The Hasso Plattner Institute of Design at Stanford University, commonly known as the d.school, is a prime example of an educational institution that successfully integrates creativity and innovation into its curriculum through PBL. The d.school offers courses that challenge students to tackle real-world problems using design thinking, a methodology that encourages empathy, ideation, and prototyping.

Students at the d.school work on interdisciplinary teams to develop innovative solutions to complex issues, ranging from healthcare to sustainability. This experience not only enhances their creative problem-solving skills but also prepares them to approach entrepreneurship with a mindset geared toward innovation and social impact (Brown, 2009).

INCORPORATING ENTREPRENEURIAL COMPETITIONS AND EVENTS

Another effective way to foster entrepreneurial mindsets is through entrepreneurial competitions and events. These initiatives provide students with platforms to showcase their ideas, receive feedback from industry experts, and gain exposure to potential investors and partners.

Competitions such as the MIT $100K Entrepreneurship Competition and the Global Student Entrepreneur Awards offer students the opportunity to pitch their business ideas to a panel of judges, network with other entrepreneurs, and win funding to support their ventures. Participation in such events can be highly motivating and provide valuable real-world experience.

Research by Morris et al. (2013) indicates that entrepreneurial competitions enhance students' entrepreneurial skills, increase their confidence, and stimulate their interest in starting their own businesses. These events also help students build networks and gain insights from experienced entrepreneurs, further supporting their entrepreneurial journey.

Integrating entrepreneurship education into the curriculum through teaching business fundamentals, financial literacy, and encouraging creativity and innovation is essential for fostering entrepreneurial mindsets among students. Project-based learning and entrepreneurial competitions provide practical experience and stimulate creative problem-solving, critical thinking, and collaboration. By equipping students with the necessary knowledge and skills, education can inspire and prepare the next generation of entrepreneurs to create opportunities and drive economic growth.

DEVELOPING KEY ENTREPRENEURIAL SKILLS

> Enhancing Critical Thinking and Problem-Solving Abilities

Critical thinking and problem-solving are essential skills for entrepreneurs, enabling them to navigate challenges, make informed decisions, and develop innovative solutions. Education systems that prioritize these skills can significantly enhance students' entrepreneurial capabilities.

TEACHING CRITICAL THINKING AND PROBLEM-SOLVING

Educational programs can enhance critical thinking and problem-solving abilities through a variety of methods. Inquiry-based learning, where students pose questions, investigate solutions, and develop conclusions, encourages deep engagement with material and fosters analytical thinking. Similarly, case studies and simulations allow students to apply theoretical knowledge to real-world scenarios, promoting strategic thinking and practical problem-solving.

Research underscores the importance of these educational strategies. A study by Abrami et al. (2015) found that students who participated in programs emphasizing critical thinking skills demonstrated significant improvements in their ability to analyze, evaluate, and synthesize information. These skills are directly transferable to entrepreneurial activities, where problem-solving and innovation are crucial for success.

BUILDING LEADERSHIP, RESILIENCE, AND ADAPTABILITY

Entrepreneurship requires strong leadership, resilience, and adaptability. Entrepreneurs must be able to lead teams, navigate setbacks, and adapt to changing market conditions. Educational programs that cultivate these traits can prepare students for the dynamic nature of entrepreneurship.

FOSTERING LEADERSHIP SKILLS

Leadership skills can be developed through various educational initiatives, such as group projects, leadership workshops, and extracurricular activities. Programs that encourage students to take on leadership roles within their schools or communities help build confidence and decision-making abilities. These experiences teach students how to motivate others, manage conflicts, and drive projects to completion.

A study by Dugan and Komives (2007) found that students who participated in leadership development programs exhibited greater leadership efficacy and a higher propensity to engage in leadership activities. This underscores the importance of integrating leadership training into educational curricula to prepare future entrepreneurs.

CULTIVATING RESILIENCE AND ADAPTABILITY

Resilience and adaptability are critical for entrepreneurs, who often face uncertainty and setbacks. Educational programs can cultivate these traits by challenging students to step out of their comfort zones and encouraging a growth mindset. Programs that emphasize resilience teach students to view failures as learning opportunities and to persist in the face of adversity.

Project-based learning, internships, and experiential education are effective ways to develop resilience and adaptability. By working on real-world projects, students learn to manage risks, adapt to new information, and recover from setbacks. Research by Duckworth et al. (2007) highlights the role of grit—passion and perseverance for long-term goals—in predicting success. Educational experiences that build resilience and adaptability equip students with the mindset needed to thrive in entrepreneurial ventures.

Babson College

Babson College, renowned for its focus on entrepreneurship education, integrates the development of critical thinking, problem-solving, leadership, resilience, and adaptability into its curriculum. Babson's experiential learning approach, which includes real-world consulting projects and start-up incubators, allows students to apply their skills in practical settings. This hands-on experience is instrumental in developing the key traits needed for entrepreneurial success (Neck et al., 2014).

Developing key entrepreneurial skills such as critical thinking, problem-solving, leadership, resilience, and adaptability is essential for fostering an entrepreneurial mindset. Educational programs that emphasize these skills prepare students to navigate the challenges of entrepreneurship and innovate in dynamic environments. By enhancing these abilities, education can inspire and equip the next generation of entrepreneurs to create meaningful and lasting impacts on their communities and the broader economy.

Case Studies of Successful

Entrepreneurs Who Have Made a Positive Impact

PROFILES OF ENTREPRENEURS OVERCOMING ADVERSITY

> Stories of Entrepreneurs Who Rose from Challenging Backgrounds

Howard Schultz

Howard Schultz, the former CEO of Starbucks, grew up in a working-class family in Brooklyn, New York. Schultz's early life was marked by financial struggles, as his father worked various low-paying jobs, often without benefits. Despite these hardships, Schultz was determined to improve his circumstances through education and hard work. He attended Northern Michigan University on a football scholarship, the first in his family to attend college.

After graduating, Schultz began his career in sales and marketing, eventually joining Starbucks, which at the time was a small chain of coffee stores in Seattle. Schultz saw the potential to create a unique customer experience by transforming Starbucks into a coffeehouse culture that he had observed in Italy. He took a significant risk by purchasing the company and expanding it into a global brand. Under Schultz's leadership, Starbucks grew from a small regional business into an international powerhouse with thousands of stores worldwide.

Schultz's success can be attributed to his vision, strategic risk-taking, and commitment to creating a positive company culture.

He focused on providing quality products and excellent customer service while also offering employees benefits such as healthcare and stock options. Schultz's journey from adversity to entrepreneurial success highlights the power of resilience, innovation, and ethical business practices (Schultz & Yang, 1997).

Daymond John

Daymond John, founder of the global fashion brand FUBU, is another entrepreneur who rose from a challenging background. Growing up in the impoverished neighborhood of Hollis, Queens, John faced financial difficulties and limited opportunities. However, he was determined to succeed and began his entrepreneurial journey by selling handmade hats on the streets of New York City.

John's breakthrough came when he noticed the growing popularity of hip-hop culture and decided to create a clothing line that resonated with this audience. He started FUBU (For Us, By Us) with just $40 in seed money and support from his mother, who mortgaged their home to fund his business. Through strategic marketing and endorsements from hip-hop artists, FUBU gained national and international recognition, eventually generating over $350 million in revenue.

John's strategies for success included identifying and capitalizing on emerging market trends, leveraging cultural influences, and maintaining a strong personal brand. He also emphasized the importance of resilience and adaptability, learning from failures and continuously innovating. John's journey from adversity to entrepreneurial success highlights the potential for individuals to create significant economic and social impact through perseverance and strategic thinking (John & Paisner, 2007).

ANALYSIS OF THE STRATEGIES THEY USED TO SUCCEED

> Leveraging Unique Market Opportunities

Both Schultz and John identified and capitalized on unique market opportunities that aligned with their personal experiences and cultural trends. Schultz transformed Starbucks into a global coffeehouse culture, while John tapped into the burgeoning hip-hop fashion scene. Their ability to connect with and understand their audiences was crucial to their success.

BUILDING STRONG PERSONAL BRANDS

A key strategy employed by both entrepreneurs was building strong personal brands. Schultz's commitment to ethical business practices and employee welfare built a loyal customer and employee base, while John's entrepreneurial journey and his role as a mentor and investor on the television show "Shark Tank" established him as a credible and influential business figure. Personal branding helped them gain visibility, attract opportunities, and create lasting legacies.

STRATEGIC RISK-TAKING AND INNOVATION

Both entrepreneurs demonstrated strategic risk-taking and innovation. Schultz took significant risks by purchasing Starbucks and expanding it globally, ventures that required substantial investment and carried high stakes. John similarly risked financial security by investing in his clothing line and pursuing unconventional marketing strategies. Their willingness to take calculated risks and innovate was instrumental in their success.

COMMITMENT TO SOCIAL IMPACT

Schultz and John both used their success to drive social impact. Schultz's philanthropic efforts include substantial donations to educational initiatives and community development projects. John's involvement in mentoring young entrepreneurs and supporting minority-owned businesses highlights his commitment to economic empowerment and community development. Their dedication to social impact underscores the potential for entrepreneurship to drive positive change beyond financial success.

The stories of Howard Schultz and Daymond John illustrate how entrepreneurs can overcome adversity and achieve remarkable success through resilience, strategic thinking, and innovation. By leveraging unique market opportunities, building strong personal brands, taking calculated risks, and committing to social impact, these entrepreneurs have made significant contributions to their industries and communities. Their journeys serve as powerful examples of how entrepreneurship can transform lives and create lasting positive impacts.

Social Entrepreneurs and Community Development

EXAMPLES OF ENTREPRENEURS ADDRESSING SOCIAL AND ENVIRONMENTAL ISSUES

Leila Janah and Samasource

Leila Janah, the founder of Samasource, dedicated her career to creating economic opportunities for impoverished communities through the power of technology and digital work. Samasource, a social enterprise, connects low-income individuals in developing countries with digital work from some of the world's largest tech companies. By providing training and employment in data entry, content moderation, and other digital tasks, Samasource helps lift people out of poverty.

Janah's vision was to leverage the internet to bridge the gap between talent and opportunity. Her model has been highly effective; according to a study by the Rockefeller Foundation, workers at Samasource experienced significant increases in income, education, and job skills, which had lasting positive impacts on their families and communities (Rockefeller Foundation, 2014). Janah's work demonstrates the transformative potential of combining entrepreneurship with technology to address global poverty.

Bunker Roy and Barefoot College

Bunker Roy founded Barefoot College in India to provide education and vocational training to rural, impoverished communities, particularly focusing on women. The college trains "barefoot" solar engineers, artisans, midwives, and doctors, enabling them to bring sustainable energy and essential services to their villages. By empowering women and leveraging traditional knowledge, Barefoot College addresses critical social and environmental issues.

Barefoot College's impact is profound; it has trained thousands of women as solar engineers, who have subsequently electrified their villages using solar power. This initiative not only promotes renewable energy but also improves living conditions and economic opportunities in remote areas. A report by the International Renewable Energy Agency (IRENA) highlights Barefoot College as a successful model of community-based sustainable development (IRENA, 2013).

Hamdi Ulukaya and Chobani

Hamdi Ulukaya, the founder of Chobani, has used his business success to drive social change, particularly in supporting refugees and immigrants. Ulukaya, originally from Turkey, immigrated to the United States and founded Chobani, which became one of the most successful yogurt brands in the country. He established the Tent Partnership for Refugees, which mobilizes businesses to improve the lives and livelihoods of refugees.

Ulukaya's initiatives have provided employment and support to thousands of refugees, integrating them into the workforce and helping them rebuild their lives. His commitment to social responsibility is evident in Chobani's inclusive hiring practices and community support programs. According to a report by the Tent Partnership, integrating refugees into the workforce boosts economic growth and fosters social cohesion (Tent Partnership for Refugees, 2019).

THE BROADER IMPACT OF THEIR VENTURES ON COMMUNITIES AND SOCIETY

Economic Empowerment and Poverty Alleviation

Social entrepreneurs like Leila Janah and Bunker Roy have significantly contributed to economic empowerment and poverty alleviation. By providing access to education, training, and employment, their initiatives create opportunities for economic self-sufficiency and sustainable development. Samasource and Barefoot College have empowered thousands of individuals to lift themselves out of poverty, demonstrating the scalability and effectiveness of these models.

ENVIRONMENTAL SUSTAINABILITY AND CORPORATE RESPONSIBILITY

Hamdi Ulukaya's work with Chobani and the Tent Partnership for Refugees highlights the importance of corporate responsibility and environmental sustainability. By promoting inclusive hiring practices and supporting refugee communities, Ulukaya's initiatives have had a positive impact on both society and the environment. His efforts encourage other businesses to adopt similar practices, promoting a more inclusive and sustainable approach to business.

SOCIAL INNOVATION AND COMMUNITY DEVELOPMENT

Social entrepreneurs drive social innovation by developing new solutions to address pressing social and environmental challenges. Initiatives like Barefoot College's training programs and Samasource's digital work opportunities lead to broader community development and improved quality of life. These innovations empower individuals and communities to become self-sufficient and resilient.

CREATING A CULTURE OF GIVING AND RESPONSIBILITY

The broader impact of social entrepreneurship extends to creating a culture of giving and responsibility. Entrepreneurs like Janah, Roy, and Ulukaya have demonstrated that businesses can be a force for good, challenging the traditional notion that profit is the sole purpose of business. Their success stories inspire other entrepreneurs to adopt socially responsible practices and contribute to their communities.

Social entrepreneurs like Leila Janah, Bunker Roy, and Hamdi

Ulukaya exemplify how entrepreneurship can address social and environmental issues while fostering community development. Their ventures have had a profound impact on poverty alleviation, environmental sustainability, and social innovation. By creating opportunities for economic empowerment and promoting responsible business practices, these entrepreneurs have made lasting contributions to their communities and society. Their stories demonstrate that entrepreneurship can be a powerful force for positive change, inspiring others to follow in their footsteps.

8

Integrating Faith and Education

The Role of Faith in Education and Personal Development

FAITH AS A FOUNDATION FOR MORAL AND ETHICAL DEVELOPMENT

> Teaching Values such as Honesty, Compassion, and Integrity

Faith-based education plays a crucial role in teaching and reinforcing core moral and ethical values such as honesty, compassion, and integrity. These values are fundamental to personal development and societal cohesion, helping individuals navigate their lives with a strong moral compass.

HONESTY

Many religious traditions emphasize the importance of honesty. For example, in Christianity, the Ten Commandments explicitly state, "You shall not bear false witness against your neighbor" (Exodus 20:16, NIV). This principle encourages individuals to value truth and transparency in their interactions. Similarly, in Islam, honesty is considered a central virtue, as highlighted in the Hadith, where the Prophet Muhammad said, "Truthfulness leads to righteousness, and righteousness leads to Paradise" (Sahih Bukhari).

Educational programs in faith-based schools often incorporate teachings from religious texts and principles to emphasize honesty. This approach helps students internalize the value of truthfulness, which is essential for building trust and integrity in personal and professional relationships. Research by Hill et al. (2000) suggests that students who receive faith-based education are more likely to exhibit honesty and ethical behavior due to the integration of religious teachings in their moral development.

COMPASSION

Compassion is another key value emphasized in faith-based education. Many religious traditions advocate for empathy and kindness towards others. In Buddhism, for example, the principle of Karuna (compassion) is central to the practice, encouraging individuals to alleviate the suffering of others. In Christianity, Jesus' teachings in the New Testament emphasize love and compassion, as seen in the parable of the Good Samaritan (Luke 10:25-37, NIV).

Faith-based schools often incorporate community service and charitable activities into their curricula to foster compassion among students. These activities not only provide practical experiences in helping others but also reinforce the importance of empathy and social responsibility. A study by Furrow et al. (2004) found that students involved in faith-based education are more likely to engage in prosocial behaviors, such as volunteering and helping others, due to the emphasis on compassion in their moral education.

Integrity

Integrity, or the quality of being honest and having strong moral principles, is a cornerstone of many religious teachings. In Hinduism, the concept of Dharma encompasses duties and ethical conduct that uphold righteousness and integrity. Similarly, in Judaism, the teachings of the Torah emphasize integrity through adherence to God's commandments and ethical living.

Faith-based education systems strive to instill integrity in students by teaching them to align their actions with their moral and ethical beliefs. This alignment is critical for developing a sense of accountability and responsibility. According to a study by Regnerus and Elder (2003), students in faith-based schools often demonstrate higher levels of integrity and ethical decision-making, attributed to the moral framework provided by their religious education.

> The Influence of Faith on Character Building and Decision-Making

Faith-based education significantly influences character building and decision-making by providing a moral framework that guides students in their personal and academic lives. This framework helps students develop a clear sense of right and wrong, making it easier for them to navigate ethical dilemmas and make principled decisions.

CHARACTER BUILDING

Religious teachings often include stories and parables that illustrate moral lessons and ethical conduct. These narratives serve as powerful tools for character building, as they provide concrete examples of virtuous behavior. For instance, the story of Rama in the Hindu epic Ramayana exemplifies virtues such as duty, honor, and righteousness. By learning about and reflecting on such stories, students develop a deeper understanding of the values that underpin strong character.

DECISION-MAKING

Faith-based education encourages students to consider the ethical implications of their decisions. Religious teachings often provide guidance on how to approach various life situations, emphasizing principles such as justice, kindness, and humility. For example, the teachings of the Quran offer comprehensive guidance on ethical living, influencing how students approach decision-making processes.

Research by Smith and Denton (2005) indicates that adolescents who actively engage in religious practices are more likely to consider the moral aspects of their decisions and seek guidance from their faith in challenging situations. This moral guidance helps them make choices that align with their values and principles, fostering a sense of integrity and accountability.

Faith-based education plays a pivotal role in teaching values such as honesty, compassion, and integrity. By integrating religious teachings into moral and ethical development, faith-based schools help students build strong character and make principled decisions. The influence of faith on education extends beyond academic achievement, shaping students into responsible and ethical individuals who contribute positively to society.

Faith in Promoting Resilience and Purpose

HOW FAITH PROVIDES A SENSE OF PURPOSE AND DIRECTION

Faith often serves as a guiding force, providing individuals with a sense of purpose and direction in life. This sense of purpose can be particularly powerful in an educational context, where students are navigating their identities and future aspirations. Faith-based education integrates spiritual beliefs and practices, helping students to find meaning and direction in their academic and personal lives.

FAITH AS A GUIDING PRINCIPLE

Religious teachings frequently emphasize the importance of leading a purposeful life. For example, in Christianity, the concept of vocation encourages individuals to understand their unique calling and to pursue it with dedication. The Bible states, "For I know the plans I have for you," declares the Lord, "plans to prosper you and not to harm you, plans to give you hope and a future" (Jeremiah 29:11, NIV). This passage reassures believers that their lives have a divine purpose, which can guide their decisions and actions.

In Islam, the principle of Tawhid (the oneness of God) emphasizes that all aspects of life, including education, should align with the worship and service of God. This belief encourages students to pursue their studies with the intention of fulfilling their spiritual and worldly responsibilities. A study by Ali and Gibbs (1998) found that Muslim students who integrated their faith into their academic pursuits reported higher levels of motivation and satisfaction, as they perceived their education as a means to serve a higher purpose.

IMPACT ON ACADEMIC AND PERSONAL GOALS

Faith-based education helps students set and achieve academic and personal goals by providing a framework for understanding their strengths, weaknesses, and aspirations. This framework often includes a strong emphasis on self-discipline, perseverance, and ethical conduct, all of which are critical for academic success. Research by Muller and Ellison (2001) suggests that students who are actively involved in their religious communities are more likely to set high academic goals and strive to achieve them, as their faith reinforces the importance of hard work and excellence.

THE ROLE OF FAITH IN HELPING STUDENTS COPE WITH CHALLENGES AND ADVERSITY

Faith plays a crucial role in helping students cope with challenges and adversity by offering emotional support, fostering resilience, and providing a sense of hope and optimism.

EMOTIONAL SUPPORT AND COMMUNITY

One of the key ways faith helps students navigate difficulties is through the emotional support and sense of community it provides. Religious communities often serve as extended families, offering encouragement, guidance, and practical assistance during times of need. This support network can be invaluable for students facing personal or academic challenges.

For instance, a study by Koenig, McCullough, and Larson (2001) found that individuals who actively participate in religious communities report higher levels of social support, which is linked to better mental health and well-being. This support helps students feel connected and understood, reducing feelings of isolation and stress.

FOSTERING RESILIENCE

Faith fosters resilience by encouraging a positive outlook and helping individuals reframe their experiences in a meaningful context. Many religious teachings emphasize the importance of perseverance and trust in a higher power during difficult times. For example, in Buddhism, the concept of Dukkha (suffering) is seen as an inherent part of life, but it is through understanding and overcoming suffering that individuals achieve enlightenment and inner peace.

Educational programs in faith-based schools often incorporate spiritual practices such as prayer, meditation, and reflection, which help students develop coping strategies and build resilience. A study by Pargament (1997) highlighted that individuals who use religious coping methods, such as seeking spiritual support and reinterpreting stressors as part of a divine plan, are more likely to experience positive psychological outcomes during stressful situations.

PROVIDING HOPE AND OPTIMISM

Faith instills a sense of hope and optimism, which is essential for overcoming adversity. Belief in a higher power and the idea that life has a meaningful purpose can inspire students to persevere through challenges. In Judaism, the concept of Tikvah (hope) is fundamental, encouraging believers to maintain a hopeful outlook despite hardships. The Talmud states, "Even if the sword is at your neck, do not despair" (Berakhot 10a), underscoring the importance of hope in Jewish teachings.

Research by Seligman and Csikszentmihalyi (2000) in the field of positive psychology supports the idea that hope and optimism are critical for psychological resilience and overall well-being. Faith-based education that promotes these virtues can significantly enhance students' ability to cope with and overcome adversity.

Faith plays a vital role in promoting resilience and providing a sense of purpose and direction in students' lives. By integrating spiritual beliefs and practices into education, faith-based schools help students navigate challenges, set and achieve goals, and find meaning in their experiences. The emotional support, resilience, and hope fostered by faith contribute to students' overall well-being and success, both academically and personally.

Inclusive Curriculum Design

STRATEGIES FOR INCORPORATING MULTIPLE FAITH PERSPECTIVES IN THE CLASSROOM

Creating an inclusive curriculum that respects diverse religious beliefs involves integrating multiple faith perspectives while emphasizing universal values. This approach not only fosters a deeper understanding and respect among students of different backgrounds but also enriches the educational experience by highlighting common ethical and moral principles.

INTEGRATING FAITH PERSPECTIVES

One effective strategy for incorporating multiple faith perspectives is to design a curriculum that includes the study of various religious traditions. This can be achieved through comparative religion courses that explore the beliefs, practices, and histories of different faiths. Such courses should be structured to highlight both the unique aspects and common values shared across religions, fostering mutual respect and understanding.

For example, a unit on compassion might include teachings from Christianity, such as the Parable of the Good Samaritan, alongside similar concepts from Buddhism (Karuna), Islam (Rahma), Hinduism (Ahimsa), and Judaism (Chesed). By presenting these perspectives side-by-side, students can appreciate the universal importance of compassion across different faiths.

GUEST SPEAKERS AND INTERFAITH DIALOGUES

Inviting guest speakers from various religious communities to share their beliefs and experiences can provide students with firsthand insights into different faiths. Interfaith dialogues, where representatives from multiple religions discuss common values and ethical dilemmas, can also be an effective educational tool. These interactions allow students to ask questions, dispel misconceptions, and build a more nuanced understanding of religious diversity.

Research by Stern (2004) suggests that interfaith education programs promote greater tolerance and reduce prejudices among students. These programs create opportunities for meaningful engagement and foster an environment of respect and inclusivity.

MULTICULTURAL AND INTERFAITH ACTIVITIES

Incorporating multicultural and interfaith activities into the school calendar can further enhance students' appreciation of religious diversity. Celebrations of various religious holidays, such as Diwali, Eid, Hanukkah, and Christmas, provide opportunities for students to learn about and participate in different cultural traditions. These activities not only educate but also create a sense of community and shared experience.

BALANCING RELIGIOUS TEACHINGS WITH SECULAR EDUCATION

While it is important to respect and incorporate religious perspectives, balancing these teachings with secular education ensures that the curriculum remains inclusive and relevant to all students, regardless of their faith background.

SECULAR ETHICS AND UNIVERSAL VALUES

One approach is to focus on secular ethics and universal values that are shared across religious traditions. Values such as honesty, respect, empathy, and justice can be taught through both religious and secular lenses. For instance, lessons on honesty can draw from religious texts like the Bible and the Quran, as well as secular ethical theories and real-world applications.

A study by Nucci and Narvaez (2008) found that integrating moral education with both religious and secular perspectives helps students develop a well-rounded understanding of ethics. This approach ensures that all students, regardless of their personal beliefs, can engage with and relate to the material.

CRITICAL THINKING AND COMPARATIVE ANALYSIS

Encouraging critical thinking and comparative analysis is another effective strategy. Students can be taught to analyze religious teachings and ethical principles critically, comparing them with secular viewpoints. This method fosters critical thinking skills and helps students appreciate the complexities of ethical decision-making.

For example, a comparative analysis of the Golden Rule—"Do unto others as you would have them do unto you"—can include its various iterations in different religions and philosophical traditions. Students can explore how this principle is interpreted and applied in different contexts, deepening their understanding of its universal significance.

INCLUSIVE LANGUAGE AND MATERIALS

Using inclusive language and materials that acknowledge and respect diverse religious beliefs is essential. Textbooks, reading materials, and classroom discussions should reflect a balanced representation of different faiths. Teachers should be mindful of their language, avoiding assumptions about students' beliefs and creating a respectful and open classroom environment.

Creating a curriculum that respects diverse religious beliefs while emphasizing universal values requires thoughtful integration of multiple faith perspectives and a balance with secular education. Strategies such as comparative religion courses, interfaith dialogues, and multicultural activities foster mutual respect and understanding among students. By focusing on secular ethics and critical thinking, educators can ensure that the curriculum is inclusive and relevant to all students. This approach not only enriches the educational experience but also prepares students to navigate a diverse and interconnected world with empathy and respect.

Emphasizing Universal Values

IDENTIFYING AND TEACHING CORE VALUES SHARED ACROSS DIFFERENT RELIGIONS

Teaching universal values that are shared across various religious traditions can create a foundation of mutual respect and understanding among students from diverse backgrounds. These core values include compassion, integrity, respect, and justice, which are emphasized in numerous religious and philosophical teachings.

COMPASSION

Compassion is a fundamental value found in many religious traditions. In Christianity, Jesus teaches the importance of loving one's neighbor as oneself (Mark 12:31, NIV). Similarly, in Buddhism, compassion (Karuna) is a key virtue, guiding individuals to alleviate the suffering of others. Islam also emphasizes compassion, with the Prophet Muhammad stating, "Show mercy to those on earth, and the One in the heavens will show mercy to you" (Sunan Abu Dawood, 4941).

To teach compassion, educators can incorporate stories, parables, and teachings from different religions that highlight compassionate acts. Discussions and reflections on these stories can help students understand the importance of empathy and kindness in their interactions with others.

INTEGRITY

Integrity is another universal value that is highly regarded across religious traditions. In Hinduism, the concept of Dharma encompasses living a life of righteousness and integrity. Judaism teaches the importance of honesty and ethical behavior through the Torah, with Proverbs 12:22 stating, "The Lord detests lying lips, but he delights in people who are trustworthy" (NIV). Similarly, Sikhism emphasizes the importance of truthful living, as stated in the Guru Granth Sahib, "Truth is the highest virtue, but higher still is truthful living."

Educators can promote integrity by discussing ethical dilemmas and encouraging students to reflect on the importance of honesty and moral principles in their daily lives. Case studies and role-playing activities can help students practice making decisions that align with their values.

RESPECT

Respect for others, regardless of their background or beliefs, is a core value in many religions. Confucianism teaches the importance of respect and filial piety, emphasizing harmonious relationships within families and communities. In Islam, respect for others is fundamental, as reflected in the Quranic verse, "O mankind, indeed We have created you from male and female and made you peoples and tribes that you may know one another" (Quran 49:13, Sahih International).

Classroom discussions on respect can include exploring different cultural practices and traditions, helping students appreciate the diversity within their communities. Encouraging respectful dialogue and active listening in the classroom fosters an environment where all students feel valued and heard.

JUSTICE

Justice is a universal value that promotes fairness and equality. In Christianity, the Bible calls for justice, as seen in Isaiah 1:17, "Learn to do right; seek justice. Defend the oppressed" (NIV). In Islam, justice is a core principle, with the Quran stating, "O you who have believed, be persistently standing firm in justice" (Quran 4:135, Sahih International). Similarly, the Bahá'í Faith emphasizes justice as essential for the establishment of a peaceful and equitable society.

Educators can teach justice through discussions on historical and contemporary social justice issues. Projects that involve community service and advocacy can help students apply the principles of justice in real-world contexts, fostering a commitment to equity and fairness.

Activities and Projects that Promote Interfaith Understanding and Respect

INTERFAITH SERVICE PROJECTS

One effective way to promote interfaith understanding and respect is through interfaith service projects. These projects bring students from different religious backgrounds together to work on community service initiatives, such as organizing food drives, environmental clean-ups, or building shelters. By collaborating on common goals, students can learn about each other's beliefs and practices while fostering a sense of unity and shared purpose.

Research by Wuthnow (2002) highlights the positive impact of interfaith service projects on fostering mutual respect and understanding. Such projects help break down stereotypes and build lasting relationships among participants from diverse backgrounds.

INTERFAITH DIALOGUES AND WORKSHOPS

Organizing interfaith dialogues and workshops can provide

students with opportunities to engage in meaningful conversations about their beliefs and values. These events can include panel discussions, guest speakers from various religious communities, and facilitated dialogues where students can ask questions and share their perspectives.

A study by Patel and Meyer (2011) found that interfaith dialogues in educational settings promote greater understanding and tolerance among students. These dialogues help students develop empathy and appreciation for the diversity of religious beliefs, fostering a more inclusive and respectful school environment.

CULTURAL EXCHANGE PROGRAMS

Cultural exchange programs that include visits to different places of worship and participation in religious and cultural celebrations can also promote interfaith understanding. These programs allow students to experience firsthand the practices and traditions of various religions, deepening their appreciation for religious diversity.

For example, students could visit a mosque, synagogue, church, or temple and learn about the religious practices and rituals observed there. Participating in celebrations like Diwali, Eid, Hanukkah, and Christmas can help students understand the significance of these events and the values they represent.

Emphasizing universal values shared across different religions in the curriculum fosters mutual respect and understanding among students from diverse backgrounds. By teaching core values such as compassion, integrity, respect, and justice, educators can create a foundation for ethical and moral development. Activities and projects that promote interfaith understanding, such as interfaith service projects, dialogues, and cultural exchange programs, further enhance students' appreciation for religious diversity and foster a more inclusive school environment.

The Impact of Faith-Based Education on Students' Lives

ACADEMIC AND PERSONAL OUTCOMES

> Research on the Academic Performance of Students in Faith-Based Schools

Faith-based education has long been recognized for its emphasis on both academic excellence and moral development. Numerous studies have shown that students in faith-based schools often outperform their peers in public schools in various academic metrics.

ACADEMIC PERFORMANCE

A study by Jeynes (2012) revealed that students attending faith-based schools generally achieve higher standardized test scores compared to their counterparts in public schools. The study found that the average academic performance of students in faith-based schools was significantly higher in subjects such as mathematics, reading, and science. This academic advantage is attributed to several factors, including smaller class sizes, a strong emphasis on discipline, and a supportive school environment that fosters a culture of learning.

Moreover, faith-based schools often provide a more rigorous curriculum that challenges students to reach their full potential. A report by the National Center for Education Statistics (NCES) indicated that students in private religious schools were more likely to complete advanced coursework in high school, which better prepares them for college and career success (NCES, 2016).

COLLEGE ENROLLMENT AND GRADUATION RATES

Faith-based schools also boast higher college enrollment and graduation rates. The Cardus Education Survey (2018) found that graduates of faith-based schools are more likely to attend and graduate from college compared to their peers from public schools. The survey highlighted that the supportive community and strong moral foundation provided by faith-based schools play a crucial role in encouraging students to pursue higher education and persist through challenges.

PERSONAL DEVELOPMENT BENEFITS

In addition to academic achievements, faith-based education significantly impacts personal development, fostering traits such as self-esteem, empathy, and social responsibility.

INCREASED SELF-ESTEEM

Faith-based education often emphasizes the inherent worth and dignity of each individual, grounded in religious teachings. This focus on self-worth can positively influence students' self-esteem. A study by Watson, Milliron, and Morris (2013) found that students in faith-based schools reported higher levels of self-esteem compared to those in non-religious schools. This increased self-esteem is linked to the supportive and nurturing environment provided by faith-based schools, where students are encouraged to develop a positive self-image and recognize their unique talents and potential.

EMPATHY AND SOCIAL RESPONSIBILITY

Empathy and social responsibility are core values in many religious teachings, and faith-based schools strive to instill these values in their students. Programs and activities that promote community service, charity, and social justice are integral parts of the curriculum in faith-based schools.

A study by Hill and Den Dulk (2013) found that students in faith-based schools are more likely to engage in volunteer work and community service compared to their peers in public schools. This engagement in altruistic activities fosters empathy and a sense of social responsibility. Students learn to appreciate the importance of helping others and contributing to the common good.

MORAL AND ETHICAL DEVELOPMENT

Faith-based education places a strong emphasis on moral and ethical development. Students are taught to adhere to a set of ethical standards and values that guide their behavior and decision-making. This moral framework helps students navigate the complexities of life with integrity and compassion.

Research by Regnerus and Uecker (2006) indicates that students from faith-based schools exhibit higher levels of ethical behavior and moral reasoning. They are more likely to make decisions that reflect their moral values and are less prone to engage in risky behaviors. The consistent reinforcement of moral principles in faith-based schools contributes to the development of well-rounded individuals who are prepared to lead ethical lives.

Faith-based education significantly impacts both the academic performance and personal development of students. Research shows that students in faith-based schools often achieve higher academic outcomes, including better standardized test scores and higher college enrollment and graduation rates. Additionally, faith-based education fosters personal development by enhancing self-esteem, empathy, and social responsibility. The strong moral and ethical foundation provided by faith-based schools prepares students to navigate life's challenges with integrity and compassion, contributing positively to their communities and society.

The Impact of Faith-Based Education on Students' Lives

COMMUNITY AND SOCIAL CONTRIBUTIONS

> Case Studies of Students from Faith-Based Schools Contributing to Their Communities

Faith-based schools emphasize not only academic excellence but also the importance of community service and social responsibility. This holistic approach to education often results in students who are deeply committed to contributing positively to their communities.

St. Ignatius High School, Cleveland, Ohio

St. Ignatius High School, a Jesuit institution in Cleveland, Ohio, has a long-standing tradition of community service. One notable program is the Saint Ignatius Arrupe Neighborhood Partnership, which involves students in various service projects in the local community. These projects include tutoring children, organizing food drives, and assisting at shelters.

A recent initiative involved students working with the Cleveland

Food Bank to address food insecurity in the area. Students organized and participated in food distribution events, providing meals to hundreds of families in need. This experience not only helped alleviate immediate hunger but also raised awareness about the issue of food insecurity among the students, fostering a sense of empathy and civic duty (St. Ignatius High School, 2020).

The Ursuline School, New Rochelle, New York

The Ursuline School in New Rochelle, New York, integrates service learning into its curriculum, encouraging students to engage in meaningful community service activities. One significant project involved students partnering with Habitat for Humanity to build affordable housing for low-income families.

Through this collaboration, students gained hands-on experience in construction while learning about the challenges faced by families struggling with housing insecurity. The project not only provided much-needed homes but also taught students the value of teamwork, perseverance, and community involvement. Many participants reported a heightened sense of social responsibility and a desire to continue volunteering in the future (The Ursuline School, 2021).

Islamic Foundation School, Villa Park, Illinois

Islamic Foundation School (IFS) in Villa Park, Illinois, encourages students to engage in service projects that benefit the broader community. One notable initiative is the annual "Day of Dignity," where students collaborate with local charities to provide essential services to homeless individuals, including meals, clothing, and healthcare.

Students at IFS take an active role in organizing and executing this event, which helps them develop leadership skills and a deep sense of empathy for the less fortunate. The experience reinforces the Islamic principles of charity (Zakat) and community service, highlighting the impact of faith-based education on fostering a commitment to social justice and humanitarian efforts (Islamic Foundation School, 2019).

Long-Term Impacts on Civic Engagement and Social Responsibility

ENHANCED CIVIC ENGAGEMENT

Research indicates that students who attend faith-based schools are more likely to be actively involved in civic and community activities throughout their lives. A study by Hill and den Dulk (2013) found that graduates of faith-based schools were more likely to vote, volunteer, and participate in community organizations compared to their peers from non-religious schools. This increased civic engagement is attributed to the emphasis on social responsibility and community involvement instilled in students during their formative years.

SUSTAINED COMMITMENT TO SOCIAL RESPONSIBILITY

The impact of faith-based education on social responsibility extends well beyond the school years. Graduates often carry the values and principles they learned into their professional and personal lives, making substantial contributions to society. A longitudinal study by Smith and Snell (2009) found that individuals who attended faith-based schools demonstrated higher levels of charitable giving, community service, and ethical business practices in their adult lives. This sustained commitment to social responsibility highlights the long-term benefits of integrating faith and education.

INFLUENCE ON PROFESSIONAL CHOICES

Faith-based education also influences students' career choices, often guiding them toward professions that allow them to serve others and contribute to the common good. Many graduates pursue careers in education, healthcare, social work, and non-profit organizations, where they can directly impact their communities. The emphasis on ethical decision-making and service in faith-based schools prepares students to navigate their professional lives with integrity and a strong sense of purpose.

Loyola University Chicago

Loyola University Chicago, a Jesuit institution, has a strong tradition of producing graduates who are committed to social justice and community service. Alumni from Loyola often engage in careers that focus on serving marginalized populations and addressing social inequities. For example, the university's graduates include numerous social workers, public health professionals, and educators who work tirelessly to improve the lives of others. This commitment to social responsibility is a testament to the impact of faith-based education on fostering a lifelong dedication to serving the common good (Loyola University Chicago, 2020).

Faith-based education significantly impacts students' community and social contributions. Through service projects, students develop a deep sense of empathy, civic engagement, and social responsibility. Case studies from institutions like St. Ignatius High School, The Ursuline School, and Islamic Foundation School demonstrate how faith-based education fosters a commitment to community service and social justice. The long-term impacts of faith-based education are evident in the sustained civic engagement, ethical decision-making, and professional choices of its graduates, who continue to contribute positively to society throughout their lives.

9

Preparing for the Future: Educating the Next Generation of Leaders

The Importance of Visionary Education in Shaping Future Leaders

THE ROLE OF VISIONARY EDUCATION IN DEVELOPING LEADERSHIP QUALITIES

Defining Visionary Education and Its Impact on Leadership

Visionary education is an educational approach that goes beyond traditional teaching methods to inspire students to think critically, innovate, and envision a better future. It focuses on fostering creativity, ethical decision-making, and a commitment to social responsibility. Visionary education aims to prepare students not just for the jobs of today but for the challenges and opportunities of tomorrow.

IMPACT ON LEADERSHIP DEVELOPMENT

Visionary education significantly impacts leadership development by instilling qualities such as foresight, innovation, and a strong moral compass in students. These qualities are essential for effective leadership in a rapidly changing world. Visionary leaders are those who can anticipate future trends, inspire others to work towards a common goal, and make ethical decisions that benefit society as a whole.

HISTORICAL EXAMPLES OF VISIONARY EDUCATION SHAPING LEADERS

Historically, visionary education has played a crucial role in shaping influential leaders who have made significant contributions to society. One notable example is the Montessori method, developed by Maria Montessori in the early 20th century. This educational approach emphasizes self-directed learning, hands-on activities, and collaborative play. Montessori education has been credited with nurturing innovative thinkers such as Larry Page and Sergey Brin, the founders of Google. Both Page and Brin have attributed their ability to think creatively and solve complex problems to their Montessori education (Said, 2013).

Another example is the Waldorf education system, founded by Rudolf Steiner. Waldorf education focuses on holistic development, integrating academic, artistic, and practical skills. It encourages students to develop their intellectual, emotional, and physical capacities harmoniously. Prominent leaders who have benefited from Waldorf education include Kenneth Chenault, former CEO of American Express, and Jens Stoltenberg, Secretary General of NATO. Their education in a Waldorf school helped them develop strong leadership qualities, such as strategic thinking and empathy (Easton, 1997).

VISIONARY EDUCATION MODELS

In contemporary settings, visionary education models continue to shape future leaders. Schools that integrate Science, Technology, Engineering, Arts, and Mathematics (STEAM) with entrepreneurship are at the forefront of this movement. These schools emphasize interdisciplinary learning, critical thinking, and real-world problem-solving, preparing students to become innovative leaders in various fields.

RESEARCH ON VISIONARY EDUCATION

Research supports the effectiveness of visionary education in developing leadership qualities. A study by the Partnership for 21st Century Skills (2010) found that students who engage in project-based learning, which is a key component of visionary education, demonstrate higher levels of critical thinking, creativity, and collaboration. These skills are crucial for leadership in the 21st century.

Furthermore, a report by the World Economic Forum (2016) highlights the importance of skills such as complex problem-solving, critical thinking, and creativity for future leaders. Visionary education, by focusing on these skills, prepares students to navigate the complexities of the modern world and lead effectively.

Visionary education plays a pivotal role in developing leadership qualities by fostering foresight, innovation, and ethical decision-making. Historical and contemporary examples demonstrate the profound impact of visionary education on shaping influential leaders. By emphasizing critical thinking, creativity, and real-world problem-solving, visionary education equips students with the skills needed to lead in a rapidly changing world. As research indicates, the qualities nurtured by visionary education are essential for effective leadership in the 21st century.

The Need for Forward-Thinking Education Models

ADDRESSING GLOBAL CHALLENGES THROUGH EDUCATION

In the 21st century, education must evolve to address the complex and interrelated global challenges that we face, such as climate change, social inequality, and economic instability. Forward-thinking education models are essential for equipping students with the knowledge and skills necessary to tackle these issues and drive sustainable development.

EDUCATION FOR SUSTAINABLE DEVELOPMENT (ESD)

Education for Sustainable Development (ESD) is an approach that integrates principles, values, and practices of sustainable development into all aspects of education and learning. ESD empowers students to make informed decisions and take responsible actions for environmental integrity, economic viability, and a just society. According to UNESCO, ESD involves key issues such as climate change, biodiversity, poverty reduction, and sustainable consumption, which are critical for shaping the future leaders who will address these global challenges (UNESCO, 2014).

For instance, schools that adopt ESD curricula often include projects on renewable energy, waste management, and conservation, encouraging students to apply their learning to real-world problems. This hands-on approach not only enhances students' understanding of sustainability issues but also fosters a sense of responsibility and agency.

GLOBAL CITIZENSHIP EDUCATION (GCED)

Global Citizenship Education (GCED) aims to equip learners with the competencies needed to navigate and thrive in a globalized world. GCED promotes values such as respect for diversity, empathy, and social justice, encouraging students to become active and responsible global citizens. The United Nations emphasizes that GCED is crucial for addressing global challenges, as it fosters an understanding of interconnectedness and promotes collective action (UN, 2015).

Programs that integrate GCED into their curricula often include studies on human rights, cultural diversity, and global governance. These programs help students develop a global perspective and understand the importance of collaboration and solidarity in addressing worldwide issues. A study by Reimers et al. (2016) found that students who participate in GCED programs are more likely to engage in civic activities and demonstrate a commitment to global justice and sustainability.

THE IMPACT OF TECHNOLOGY AND GLOBALIZATION ON EDUCATION

> Leveraging Technology for Enhanced Learning

Technology has a profound impact on education, offering innovative tools and resources that enhance learning experiences and expand access to knowledge. The integration of technology in education, often referred to as EdTech, includes digital classrooms, online courses, and interactive learning platforms that cater to diverse learning styles and needs.

BLENDED AND ONLINE LEARNING

Blended learning, which combines traditional classroom instruction with online learning, provides a flexible and personalized educational experience. Research by Means et al. (2013) indicates that students in blended learning environments tend to perform better academically compared to those in traditional settings. Online learning platforms, such as Khan Academy and Coursera, offer a wide range of courses that allow students to learn at their own pace and explore subjects beyond the standard curriculum.

STEM AND STEAM EDUCATION

The focus on Science, Technology, Engineering, and Mathematics (STEM) education, and its expansion to include the Arts (STEAM), is crucial for preparing students for the future workforce. These programs emphasize critical thinking, creativity, and problem-solving skills, which are essential in a technology-driven world. According to a report by the U.S. Department of Education,

STEM education fosters innovation and economic growth, making it a priority for educational institutions globally (USDOE, 2016).

GLOBALIZATION AND CROSS-CULTURAL LEARNING

Globalization has made the world more interconnected, and education systems must adapt to prepare students for this reality. Cross-cultural learning experiences, such as study abroad programs, international collaborations, and virtual exchanges, provide students with the opportunity to engage with diverse perspectives and develop intercultural competencies.

INTERNATIONAL BACCALAUREATE (IB) PROGRAM

The International Baccalaureate (IB) program is an example of an educational framework that promotes global awareness and intercultural understanding. The IB curriculum encourages students to think critically, reflect on their learning, and engage with complex global issues. A study by Conley and Ward (2009) found that IB students are better prepared for the demands of higher education and exhibit higher levels of global competence compared to their peers.

DIGITAL LITERACY AND LIFELONG LEARNING

In a rapidly changing world, digital literacy and the ability to learn continuously are essential skills. Education systems must emphasize the importance of digital literacy, teaching students how to navigate and critically evaluate information in the digital age. Additionally, fostering a mindset of lifelong learning prepares students to adapt to new technologies and evolving career landscapes.

Forward-thinking education models are essential for addressing global challenges and preparing students for a rapidly changing world. By integrating Education for Sustainable Development (ESD) and Global Citizenship Education (GCED), schools can empower students to become responsible global citizens who can tackle pressing issues such as climate change and social inequality. The impact of technology and globalization on education highlights the need for blended learning, STEM and STEAM education, cross-cultural experiences, and digital literacy. These approaches ensure that the next generation of leaders is equipped with the knowledge, skills, and values necessary to navigate and thrive in the complexities of the 21st century.

Skills and Values Essential for Future Leaders

CRITICAL SKILLS FOR FUTURE LEADERS

Problem-Solving and Critical Thinking

Problem-solving and critical thinking are foundational skills for future leaders. These skills enable individuals to analyze complex situations, identify underlying issues, and develop effective solutions. In a rapidly changing world, the ability to think critically and solve problems is more important than ever.

DEVELOPING PROBLEM-SOLVING SKILLS

Educational institutions play a crucial role in nurturing problem-solving abilities. By incorporating project-based learning and real-world challenges into the curriculum, schools can encourage students to apply their knowledge in practical settings. For example, the PISA (Programme for International Student Assessment) tests, which assess students' ability to solve real-world problems, have shown that students who engage in problem-based learning outperform their peers in problem-solving tasks (OECD, 2014).

ENHANCING CRITICAL THINKING

Critical thinking involves evaluating information objectively, recognizing biases, and making reasoned judgments. Schools can foster critical thinking by encouraging debate, analysis, and reflection. Courses in philosophy, logic, and ethics, as well as activities like mock trials and debates, help students develop these skills. Research by Abrami et al. (2015) indicates that students who receive explicit instruction in critical thinking demonstrate significant improvements in their reasoning abilities and academic performance.

COMMUNICATION AND COLLABORATION

Effective communication and collaboration are essential for leadership, as they enable leaders to convey their vision, motivate teams, and work effectively with diverse groups. In an interconnected world, the ability to communicate clearly and collaborate across cultural and organizational boundaries is critical.

BUILDING COMMUNICATION SKILLS

Schools can enhance students' communication skills through activities that promote public speaking, writing, and digital literacy. Speech and debate clubs, writing workshops, and multimedia projects provide opportunities for students to practice and refine their communication abilities. A study by Darling-Hammond et al. (2008) found that students who engage in communication-focused activities are better prepared for the demands of the modern workforce.

FOSTERING COLLABORATION

Collaboration involves working effectively with others to achieve common goals. Schools can encourage collaboration through group projects, team sports, and extracurricular activities. Collaborative learning environments, where students work together to solve problems and complete tasks, help build teamwork skills. According to Johnson and Johnson (2009), cooperative learning experiences enhance students' interpersonal skills, academic achievement, and motivation.

ADAPTABILITY AND RESILIENCE

Adaptability and resilience are crucial for leaders to navigate uncertainty and overcome challenges. These skills enable individuals to adjust to changing circumstances, recover from setbacks, and maintain a positive outlook.

CULTIVATING ADAPTABILITY

Adaptability involves being open to new ideas, embracing change, and learning continuously. Schools can promote adaptability by exposing students to diverse perspectives, encouraging exploration, and integrating technology into the classroom. Programs that emphasize interdisciplinary learning and real-world applications help students develop the flexibility needed to adapt to various situations. A report by the Institute for the Future (2011) highlights the importance of adaptability in preparing students for careers that may not yet exist.

BUILDING RESILIENCE

Resilience is the ability to persevere in the face of adversity and bounce back from failures. Schools can build resilience by creating a supportive environment, teaching coping strategies, and providing opportunities for students to face and overcome challenges. Activities such as outdoor education, service learning, and mentorship programs help students develop resilience. Research by Duckworth et al. (2007) on grit—defined as passion and perseverance for long-term goals—indicates that resilience is a key predictor of success in various domains.

Developing critical skills such as problem-solving, critical thinking, communication, collaboration, adaptability, and resilience is essential for preparing the next generation of leaders. Educational institutions play a vital role in nurturing these skills through innovative teaching methods, real-world applications, and supportive learning environments. By focusing on these critical skills, schools can equip students with the tools they need to navigate the complexities of the modern world and lead effectively.

Core Values for Ethical Leadership

INTEGRITY AND ACCOUNTABILITY

Integrity and accountability are foundational values for ethical leadership. These values ensure that leaders act with honesty, transparency, and a strong moral compass, fostering trust and respect among their followers.

INTEGRITY IN LEADERSHIP

Integrity involves adhering to moral and ethical principles, even when it is challenging. Leaders with integrity are consistent in their actions, values, and beliefs, which builds trust within their organizations and communities. Integrity is crucial for making ethical decisions and guiding others toward ethical behavior.

Educational institutions can foster integrity by integrating ethics and moral reasoning into the curriculum. Case studies, ethical dilemmas, and discussions about historical and contemporary leaders who exemplify integrity can help students understand its importance. Research by Simons (2002) highlights that leaders who demonstrate integrity are more likely to inspire trust and commitment from their followers.

ACCOUNTABILITY IN LEADERSHIP

Accountability means being responsible for one's actions and decisions and being willing to answer for their consequences. Leaders who hold themselves accountable set a positive example for others and create a culture of responsibility and transparency. Accountability ensures that leaders remain committed to their values and the goals of their organization or community.

Schools can promote accountability by encouraging students to take responsibility for their actions, participate in self-assessment activities, and engage in collaborative projects where accountability is shared. A study by Bovens (2007) found that accountability mechanisms in educational settings lead to improved performance and ethical behavior among students.

EMPATHY AND SOCIAL RESPONSIBILITY

Empathy and social responsibility are essential for ethical leadership, as they involve understanding and addressing the needs and concerns of others. These values promote a compassionate and inclusive approach to leadership.

EMPATHY IN LEADERSHIP

Empathy is the ability to understand and share the feelings of others. Leaders with empathy can connect with their followers, build strong relationships, and create a supportive environment. Empathy allows leaders to make decisions that consider the well-being of others and address their needs effectively.

Educational programs can cultivate empathy through activities that promote perspective-taking and emotional intelligence. Role-playing, community service, and reflective practices help students develop empathy. According to research by Goleman (1995), leaders with high emotional intelligence, including empathy, are more effective in managing teams and fostering positive organizational cultures.

SOCIAL RESPONSIBILITY IN LEADERSHIP

Social responsibility involves acting in the best interest of society and contributing to the common good. Leaders who prioritize social responsibility address social, environmental, and economic issues, ensuring that their actions benefit both their organizations and the broader community.

Schools can emphasize social responsibility by incorporating service learning and community engagement into the curriculum. These experiences allow students to apply their knowledge and skills to real-world problems, fostering a sense of responsibility and civic duty. A study by Astin et al. (2000) found that students who participate in service learning develop stronger commitments to social responsibility and community engagement.

INNOVATION AND LIFELONG LEARNING

Innovation and lifelong learning are critical for leaders to adapt to changing environments and drive progress. These values encourage leaders to embrace new ideas, continuously improve their skills, and remain open to learning throughout their lives.

INNOVATION IN LEADERSHIP

Innovation involves generating new ideas, approaches, and solutions to challenges. Innovative leaders foster a culture of creativity and experimentation, encouraging their teams to think outside the box and explore new possibilities. Innovation is essential for addressing complex problems and driving organizational success.

Educational institutions can promote innovation by encouraging creative thinking, problem-solving, and interdisciplinary learning. Programs that emphasize STEAM (Science, Technology, Engineering, Arts, and Mathematics) education and entrepreneurship prepare students to become innovative leaders. Research by Dyer et al. (2011) shows that innovative leaders possess traits such as curiosity, experimentation, and a willingness to take risks.

LIFELONG LEARNING IN LEADERSHIP

Lifelong learning involves continuously seeking knowledge and self-improvement. Leaders who are committed to lifelong learning stay current with industry trends, expand their expertise, and adapt to new challenges. Lifelong learning fosters personal and professional growth, ensuring that leaders remain effective and relevant.

Schools can instill a love for learning by encouraging curiosity, critical thinking, and a growth mindset. Providing opportunities for professional development, mentorship, and ongoing education supports lifelong learning. A study by Kolb (1984) emphasizes the importance of experiential learning in fostering a continuous learning mindset, which is crucial for leadership development.

Integrity and accountability, empathy and social responsibility, and innovation and lifelong learning are core values essential for ethical leadership. Educational institutions play a vital role in nurturing these values through targeted programs and experiences. By fostering integrity, promoting empathy, encouraging social responsibility, and supporting innovation and lifelong learning, schools can prepare the next generation of leaders to navigate the complexities of the modern world with ethical principles and visionary insight.

1. Examples from AA STEAM & Entrepreneurship Academy's Approach

Innovative Curriculum and Teaching Methods

INTEGRATION OF STEAM AND ENTREPRENEURSHIP EDUCATION

At AA STEAM & Entrepreneurship Academy, we understand that education must evolve to meet the needs of the 21st century. Our innovative curriculum seamlessly integrates Science, Technology, Engineering, Arts, and Mathematics (STEAM) with entrepreneurship education, a unique approach we term "Steampreneurship." This methodology goes beyond traditional learning to encompass the understanding of existing businesses and the creation of new ventures, aligned with Georgia Standards.

STEAM INTEGRATION

STEAM education at our academy is designed to foster creativity, critical thinking, and problem-solving skills. By integrating arts into the STEM framework, we encourage students to see the connections between disciplines and apply their learning in creative ways. For example, students might design a sustainable product, incorporating principles from engineering and environmental science, and then create a marketing campaign using digital arts and media.

ENTREPRENEURSHIP EDUCATION

Entrepreneurship education at AA STEAM & Entrepreneurship Academy is about more than just starting businesses; it's about cultivating an entrepreneurial mindset. Students learn to identify opportunities, take calculated risks, and develop innovative solutions to real-world problems. Our curriculum includes lessons on financial literacy, business ethics, and economic principles, providing students with a comprehensive understanding of the entrepreneurial landscape.

PROJECT-BASED LEARNING AND REAL-WORLD APPLICATIONS

Project-based learning (PBL) is at the heart of our educational approach. PBL allows students to engage in hands-on, real-world projects that are both meaningful and educational. Through these projects, students apply what they have learned in the classroom to solve real problems, making their education relevant and impactful.

STEAMPRENEURSHIP IN ACTION

Imagine a learning environment where students are not just memorizing dates and formulas but are deeply engaged in understanding the global marketplace. At AA STEAM & Entrepreneurship Academy, students see firsthand how the clothes they wear, the gadgets they use, and the food they eat are interconnected across continents. This approach brings education to life, showing students the relevance of their learning.

INTERDISCIPLINARY EXPERIENTIAL ENTREPRENEURSHIP CURRICULUM

Our bold and transformative mission is to awaken the innate curiosity of our students and equip them with the skills to not just participate in the world, but to change it. Through our Interdisciplinary Experiential Entrepreneurship curriculum, students from grades 4 through 12 learn by doing. They follow a product from conception to market, understand the economic forces that shape our lives, and see the impact of their learning in real-time.

For example, a project might involve students designing a new eco-friendly product. They would start with market research, develop prototypes, and create business plans. They would also learn about supply chains, marketing strategies, and financial management. This comprehensive project not only teaches them about entrepreneurship but also integrates lessons from science, technology, engineering, arts, and mathematics.

IMPACT ON STUDENTS

Our innovative approach prepares students to think critically, act collaboratively, and navigate the complexities of the modern world. By engaging in interdisciplinary projects, students develop a deeper understanding of the interconnectedness of different fields and the importance of collaboration. They also learn to apply their knowledge in practical ways, preparing them for future careers and entrepreneurial ventures.

EDUCATIONAL OUTCOMES

Research supports the effectiveness of our approach. A study by the Buck Institute for Education (2018) found that students engaged in project-based learning demonstrated higher levels of academic achievement and improved problem-solving skills compared to their peers in traditional educational settings. Additionally, the integration of entrepreneurship education has been shown to enhance students' creativity, resilience, and economic understanding (European Commission, 2013).

AA STEAM & Entrepreneurship Academy is poised to become a beacon of innovation in education. Our commitment to integrating STEAM and entrepreneurship education through project-based learning prepares students not just for exams, but for life. We build leaders, innovators, and responsible global citizens, equipped to meet the challenges of tomorrow with confidence. This is our legacy, and with your support, it will continue to inspire future generations.

Building a Culture of Leadership and Service

PROGRAMS AND INITIATIVES PROMOTING LEADERSHIP DEVELOPMENT

At AA STEAM & Entrepreneurship Academy, we are committed to cultivating a culture of leadership that empowers students to become proactive, innovative, and responsible leaders. Leadership development is integrated into every aspect of our educational model, through specialized programs and initiatives that encourage students to take on leadership roles both in and outside the classroom.

LEADERSHIP ACADEMIES AND WORKSHOPS

One key component of our leadership development program includes leadership academies and workshops that focus on building essential leadership skills such as decision-making, ethical reasoning, and public speaking. These workshops are often led by experienced leaders from various sectors, providing students with mentorship and real-world insights. A study by Murphy and Johnson (2011) found that leadership programs that incorporate mentoring and practical leadership exercises significantly enhance students' leadership capabilities and self-confidence.

STUDENT LEADERSHIP COUNCILS

We also promote leadership through Student Leadership Councils, where students are given responsibilities to organize school events, manage projects, and represent their peers in school decisions. This hands-on approach not only develops leadership skills but also instills a sense of responsibility and pride in contributing to the school community. Research by Bandura (2001) on self-efficacy supports the effectiveness of such participatory experiences in building leadership qualities, as students learn to navigate challenges and achieve goals through active involvement.

COMMUNITY ENGAGEMENT AND SERVICE LEARNING PROJECTS

Community engagement and service learning are fundamental to our curriculum, reflecting our commitment to service and the development of compassionate leaders. These projects link academic curriculum to real-life community challenges, allowing students to apply their learning in meaningful ways.

SERVICE LEARNING INTEGRATION

Service learning projects at AA STEAM & Entrepreneurship Academy are carefully designed to align with academic objectives while addressing community needs. For example, students may engage in environmental projects that involve testing local water sources and presenting their findings to community stakeholders. These projects not only enhance students' understanding of environmental science but also foster skills in research, teamwork, and public communication.

PARTNERSHIPS WITH LOCAL ORGANIZATIONS

We actively partner with local non-profits, businesses, and government agencies to offer students opportunities to engage in community service. These partnerships provide platforms for students to work on larger projects, such as community clean-ups, food drives, or assisting in local shelters. According to Astin and Sax (1998), students who participate in service projects that are integrated with their coursework show increased academic development, civic responsibility, and life skills.

IMPACT OF SERVICE LEARNING

The impact of integrating service learning into our curriculum is profound. Students not only gain a deeper understanding of societal issues but also develop empathy and a lifelong commitment to service. A comprehensive study by Eyler et al. (2001) on the impact of service learning found that students who engage in service learning are more likely to exhibit increased social responsibility and commitment to service later in life. These students also develop strong problem-solving skills, as they learn to apply academic knowledge to real-world problems.

Building a culture of leadership and service at AA STEAM & Entrepreneurship Academy involves a holistic approach that combines leadership development programs with community engagement and service learning projects. By providing students with opportunities to lead, serve, and apply their learning in meaningful ways, we are preparing them to be the innovators and leaders of tomorrow. Our students are not just prepared to meet the challenges of the future; they are equipped to change the world for the better, embodying our mission of cultivating creative thinkers, problem solvers, and career innovators.

10

Vision for a Brighter World

Your Vision for the Future of Education and Society

THE ROLE OF EDUCATION IN SHAPING A BRIGHTER FUTURE

Emphasizing Holistic Development and Lifelong Learning

The future of education must prioritize holistic development and lifelong learning to prepare individuals for the complexities of the modern world. Holistic development encompasses the intellectual, emotional, social, and physical growth of students, ensuring they are well-rounded individuals capable of critical thinking, emotional intelligence, and resilience.

HOLISTIC DEVELOPMENT

Holistic education goes beyond academic excellence to nurture the overall well-being and personal growth of students. This approach integrates various aspects of learning, including emotional and social skills, creativity, physical health, and ethical values. According to Miller (2000), holistic education helps students develop a sense of purpose and interconnectedness, fostering their ability to contribute meaningfully to society.

Schools can implement holistic education by incorporating activities such as mindfulness practices, physical education, arts, and social-emotional learning (SEL) into their curricula. Research by Durlak et al. (2011) demonstrates that SEL programs significantly improve students' social skills, attitudes, behavior, and academic performance. These programs teach students to manage their emotions, set positive goals, show empathy for others, establish healthy relationships, and make responsible decisions.

LIFELONG LEARNING

Lifelong learning is the continuous pursuit of knowledge and skills throughout an individual's life. It is essential for personal and professional development, especially in a rapidly changing world where new technologies and challenges emerge constantly. Lifelong learning promotes adaptability, innovation, and a growth mindset.

Educational institutions can foster lifelong learning by encouraging curiosity and a love for learning from an early age. Providing diverse learning opportunities, such as online courses, workshops, and community programs, helps individuals continue their education beyond formal schooling. A study by the OECD (2019) found that individuals who engage in lifelong learning are better equipped to adapt to changes in the labor market and are more likely to participate in civic and social activities.

CREATING INCLUSIVE AND EQUITABLE LEARNING ENVIRONMENTS

Inclusive and equitable education is critical for ensuring that all students have the opportunity to succeed, regardless of their background or circumstances. Creating such environments involves addressing systemic barriers, promoting diversity, and ensuring that all students feel valued and supported.

INCLUSIVE EDUCATION

Inclusive education ensures that all students, including those with disabilities, learning differences, and diverse cultural backgrounds, can participate fully in the learning process. This approach requires adapting teaching methods, materials, and assessments to meet the diverse needs of students. According to the United Nations (2016), inclusive education promotes social cohesion and reduces discrimination, leading to better educational and social outcomes for all students.

To create inclusive classrooms, teachers can employ Universal Design for Learning (UDL) principles, which provide multiple means of representation, engagement, and expression. This approach allows students to access the curriculum in ways that suit their individual learning styles and needs. Research by CAST (2018) shows that UDL improves student engagement and achievement by accommodating diverse learners.

EQUITABLE EDUCATION

Equity in education involves providing all students with the resources and support they need to succeed, recognizing that different students have different needs. This approach aims to close achievement gaps and ensure that every student has access to high-quality education.

Schools can promote equity by implementing targeted interventions for students who are at risk of falling behind, such as tutoring programs, mentoring, and additional academic support. Additionally, policies that address socio-economic disparities, such as providing free meals, transportation, and access to technology, are essential for leveling the playing field. A report by the Education Trust (2018) highlights the importance of equitable funding and resources in improving educational outcomes for disadvantaged students.

The role of education in shaping a brighter future lies in emphasizing holistic development and lifelong learning, as well as creating inclusive and equitable learning environments. By fostering the intellectual, emotional, social, and physical growth of students, and by promoting continuous learning and adaptability, education can prepare individuals to navigate and contribute to an ever-changing world. Moreover, ensuring that all students have the opportunity to succeed, regardless of their background, is essential for building a just and prosperous society. Through these efforts, we can cultivate a generation of leaders, innovators, and compassionate citizens ready to face the challenges of tomorrow.

Societal Transformation Through Education

EMPOWERING INDIVIDUALS TO CONTRIBUTE TO SOCIETAL PROGRESS

Education is a powerful tool for empowering individuals to contribute meaningfully to societal progress. By equipping students with the knowledge, skills, and values necessary for active citizenship, education fosters a sense of responsibility and a commitment to improving the world.

CIVIC EDUCATION AND ENGAGEMENT

Civic education is essential for empowering individuals to participate effectively in democratic processes and community life. This type of education teaches students about their rights and responsibilities as citizens, the workings of government, and the importance of civic participation. According to a study by the Center for Information & Research on Civic Learning and Engagement (CIRCLE, 2013), students who receive comprehensive civic education are more likely to vote, engage in community service, and participate in civic activities.

SKILL DEVELOPMENT FOR SOCIETAL IMPACT

In addition to civic education, developing practical skills is crucial for enabling individuals to contribute to societal progress. Skills such as critical thinking, problem-solving, and collaboration are vital for addressing complex social challenges. A report by the World

Economic Forum (2015) emphasizes that these skills are essential for the future workforce, which will need to navigate a rapidly changing global landscape.

> Fostering Global Citizenship and Sustainable Development

GLOBAL CITIZENSHIP EDUCATION (GCED)

Global Citizenship Education (GCED) aims to cultivate a sense of global responsibility and solidarity among students. It encourages learners to appreciate cultural diversity, understand global issues, and engage in actions that contribute to a more just and sustainable world. According to UNESCO (2015), GCED is essential for preparing students to address global challenges such as climate change, inequality, and conflict.

Students engage in discussions about global interdependence, human rights, and environmental sustainability. These activities help students develop a global perspective and recognize their role in creating a better world.

EDUCATION FOR SUSTAINABLE DEVELOPMENT (ESD)

Education for Sustainable Development (ESD) integrates principles of sustainability into teaching and learning. It empowers students to make informed decisions and take responsible actions for environmental integrity, economic viability, and social equity. The United Nations Decade of Education for Sustainable Development (2005-2014) highlighted the importance of ESD in achieving sustainable development goals (UNESCO, 2014).

Our academy's commitment to ESD is reflected in projects that address sustainability issues, such as reducing waste, conserving energy, and protecting biodiversity. For instance, students might conduct research on local environmental challenges and develop action plans to mitigate their impact. These projects not only enhance students' understanding of sustainability but also encourage them to become advocates for environmental stewardship.

BUILDING A SUSTAINABLE FUTURE

Education plays a crucial role in building a sustainable future by fostering the values and skills needed for sustainable living. According to a report by the Global Education Monitoring (GEM) Report (2016), education is a key driver of progress towards sustainable development. It equips individuals with the knowledge and competencies to promote sustainability in their personal and professional lives.

Through Global Citizenship Education and Education for Sustainable Development, we can cultivate a sense of global responsibility and equip students with the knowledge and skills needed for sustainable living. Education is not just about academic achievement; it is about preparing individuals to create a brighter, more just, and sustainable world.

Practical Steps to Implement These Ideas in Schools and Communities

Curriculum and Pedagogical Innovations

INTEGRATING INTERDISCIPLINARY AND EXPERIENTIAL LEARNING APPROACHES

Integrating interdisciplinary and experiential learning approaches is crucial for creating an education system that prepares students for the complexities of the modern world. These methods encourage students to make connections across various subjects, apply their knowledge in real-world contexts, and develop critical thinking and problem-solving skills.

INTERDISCIPLINARY LEARNING

Interdisciplinary learning involves blending concepts and skills from multiple subject areas to provide a more holistic understanding of complex issues. This approach mirrors the interconnected nature of the real world, where problems and solutions often span multiple disciplines. According to a study by Jacobs (1989), interdisciplinary learning enhances students' cognitive abilities by encouraging them to see relationships and make connections between different areas of knowledge.

EXPERIENTIAL LEARNING

Experiential learning is a hands-on approach that allows students to learn by doing. This method emphasizes active participation and reflection, helping students to internalize and apply what they have learned. Kolb's Experiential Learning Theory (1984) posits that knowledge is created through the transformation of experience, and that learning is most effective when it involves a cycle of concrete experience, reflective observation, abstract conceptualization, and active experimentation.

Our curriculum incorporates various experiential learning opportunities, such as internships, lab experiments, field trips, and community service projects. For example, students might participate in a local business internship where they apply their classroom knowledge to real-world business challenges. This not only reinforces their academic learning but also helps them develop practical skills and professional networks.

EMPHASIZING DIGITAL LITERACY AND CRITICAL THINKING SKILLS

In the digital age, digital literacy and critical thinking are essential skills for students to navigate and succeed in a technology-driven world. These skills enable students to critically evaluate information, use digital tools effectively, and solve complex problems.

DIGITAL LITERACY

Digital literacy involves the ability to use technology competently, understand digital content, and communicate effectively in a digital environment. The International Society for Technology in Education (ISTE, 2016) outlines standards for students to become empowered learners, digital citizens, knowledge constructors, innovative designers, computational thinkers, creative communicators, and global collaborators.

CRITICAL THINKING SKILLS

Critical thinking involves analyzing information objectively, evaluating evidence, and making reasoned judgments. It is a crucial skill for problem-solving and decision-making in both academic and real-world contexts. A study by Abrami et al. (2015) found that critical thinking instruction significantly improves students' reasoning abilities and academic performance.

Our pedagogical approach encourages critical thinking through inquiry-based learning, Socratic questioning, and debate. For example, students might engage in a debate on a controversial topic, where they must research evidence, construct logical arguments, and defend their positions. This process helps students develop their analytical skills and learn to approach problems systematically and thoughtfully.

IMPLEMENTATION STRATEGIES

To effectively integrate interdisciplinary and experiential learning, as well as digital literacy and critical thinking, schools can adopt several strategies:

1. **Professional Development for Educators**: Provide training for teachers on interdisciplinary teaching methods, experiential learning techniques, and the integration of digital tools in the classroom. This ensures that educators are equipped to implement these innovative approaches effectively (Darling-Hammond et al., 2017).
2. **Collaborative Learning Environments**: Create collaborative spaces where students can work together on interdisciplinary projects and share their learning experiences. This fosters

teamwork and encourages the exchange of ideas (Johnson & Johnson, 2009).
3. **Technology Integration**: Incorporate technology into all aspects of the curriculum, from research and presentations to interactive simulations and virtual field trips. This helps students develop digital literacy skills in a variety of contexts (ISTE, 2016).
4. **Real-World Connections**: Partner with local businesses, community organizations, and universities to provide students with real-world learning experiences. These partnerships can offer internships, mentorships, and project-based learning opportunities that connect classroom learning to practical applications (Krajcik & Blumenfeld, 2006).

Integrating interdisciplinary and experiential learning approaches, alongside emphasizing digital literacy and critical thinking skills, is essential for preparing students to thrive in the modern world. By adopting these innovative curricular and pedagogical strategies, schools can create dynamic learning environments that foster critical thinking, creativity, and practical skills. These efforts not only enhance academic achievement but also empower students to become effective problem-solvers, ethical digital citizens, and lifelong learners ready to contribute to a brighter future.

Building Partnerships and Community Engagement

COLLABORATING WITH LOCAL ORGANIZATIONS AND BUSINESSES

Collaboration between schools and local organizations or businesses can significantly enhance educational outcomes and provide students with real-world learning opportunities. These partnerships can bring additional resources, expertise, and experiences into the classroom, enriching the curriculum and making education more relevant to students' lives.

BENEFITS OF SCHOOL-BUSINESS PARTNERSHIPS

Partnerships between schools and businesses offer numerous benefits. They can provide students with hands-on experiences, mentorship, and exposure to various career paths. According to a report by the National Association of Secondary School Principals (NASSP, 2016), effective school-business partnerships can enhance student learning, improve graduation rates, and better prepare students for the workforce.

For example, businesses can offer internships and job shadowing opportunities, allowing students to gain practical experience in their fields of interest. These experiences help students understand the skills and knowledge required for different careers and can motivate them to pursue further education and training.

CASE STUDIES OF SUCCESSFUL COLLABORATIONS

Several successful models of school-business partnerships highlight the impact of these collaborations. One notable example is the IBM P-TECH (Pathways in Technology Early College High School) program, which partners with schools to provide students with a six-year integrated high school and college curriculum focused on STEM fields. Students graduate with both a high school diploma and an associate degree, as well as workplace experience and mentoring from IBM professionals. This program has shown impressive results, with higher graduation rates and increased college enrollment among participants (IBM, 2020).

Another example is the partnership between the Boston Public Schools and local biotech companies, which offers students internships and project-based learning experiences in biotechnology. This collaboration provides students with access to state-of-the-art labs and professional mentors, enhancing their understanding of science and technology and inspiring them to pursue careers in these fields (Boston Public Schools, 2019).

Strategies for Building Effective Partnerships

To build effective partnerships with local organizations and businesses, schools should adopt several strategies:

1. **Identify Common Goals**: Establish partnerships based on shared goals and mutual benefits. Schools and businesses should work together to identify areas where their interests align and how they can support each other's objectives (Sanders, 2014).

2. **Develop Clear Agreements**: Create clear agreements outlining the roles and responsibilities of each partner. This helps ensure that both parties understand their commitments and can work together effectively (Bryson, Crosby, & Stone, 2015).
3. **Foster Open Communication**: Maintain open lines of communication to address any challenges and celebrate successes. Regular meetings and updates can help keep the partnership on track and ensure that both parties are meeting their goals (Sanders, 2014).
4. **Evaluate and Adapt**: Continuously evaluate the partnership's impact and make necessary adjustments. Collecting data on student outcomes and program effectiveness can help partners refine their approach and maximize the benefits of the collaboration (Bryson, Crosby, & Stone, 2015).

ENCOURAGING PARENTAL INVOLVEMENT AND SUPPORT

Parental involvement is a critical component of student success. Research consistently shows that students perform better academically and socially when their parents are engaged in their education (Henderson & Mapp, 2002). Schools can take several steps to encourage and support parental involvement.

CREATING A WELCOMING ENVIRONMENT

Schools should strive to create a welcoming environment for parents, making them feel valued and respected as partners in their children's education. This can include hosting regular parent-teacher conferences, providing translation services for non-English-speaking families, and ensuring that communication is clear and accessible (Henderson & Mapp, 2002).

PROVIDING OPPORTUNITIES FOR INVOLVEMENT

Offering a variety of opportunities for parents to get involved can help engage a diverse group of families. This can range from volunteering in the classroom or on field trips to participating in school governance through parent-teacher associations (PTAs) or school councils. Schools can also provide workshops and resources to help parents support their children's learning at home (Epstein, 2011).

BUILDING STRONG HOME-SCHOOL PARTNERSHIPS

Strong home-school partnerships are built on trust, respect, and open communication. Schools should actively seek input from parents and involve them in decision-making processes. Regular communication through newsletters, emails, and social media can keep parents informed and engaged in school activities (Epstein, 2011).

SUPPORTING PARENTAL EDUCATION

Providing education and resources for parents can empower them to support their children's learning more effectively. This can include offering workshops on topics such as literacy, homework help, and college readiness. Schools can also connect parents with community resources, such as adult education programs and family support services (Henderson & Mapp, 2002).

Building partnerships with local organizations and businesses, as well as encouraging parental involvement, are essential strategies for enhancing educational outcomes and creating a supportive learning environment. Effective school-business collaborations provide students with real-world experiences and mentorship, preparing them for future careers. Engaging parents in their children's education fosters academic success and social development. By implementing these strategies, schools can create a network of support that empowers students to achieve their full potential and contribute to a brighter future.

Mobilizing Educators and School Leaders

PROFESSIONAL DEVELOPMENT AND CONTINUOUS LEARNING FOR EDUCATORS

Professional development and continuous learning are essential for educators to stay current with the latest educational research, teaching strategies, and technological advancements. Investing in ongoing professional growth ensures that teachers can provide high-quality, innovative instruction that meets the needs of all students.

IMPORTANCE OF PROFESSIONAL DEVELOPMENT

Effective professional development programs are those that are sustained, collaborative, and focused on improving teachers' instructional practices. Research by Darling-Hammond et al. (2017) emphasizes that professional development should be directly linked to classroom practice and include opportunities for teachers to observe and reflect on their teaching. This helps educators integrate new strategies into their teaching and improve student outcomes.

> Types of Professional Development

1. **Workshops and Seminars**: Workshops and seminars provide opportunities for educators to learn about new teaching strategies, curriculum developments, and educational technologies. These sessions can be tailored to address specific needs and interests of teachers, making them relevant and practical.
2. **Peer Collaboration**: Collaborative professional development, such as professional learning communities (PLCs), allows teachers to work together to share ideas, solve problems, and support each other's growth. According to Vescio, Ross, and Adams (2008), PLCs are effective in fostering a culture of continuous improvement and enhancing teacher effectiveness.
3. **Coaching and Mentoring**: Personalized coaching and mentoring programs provide one-on-one support for teachers, helping them to refine their skills and implement new teaching practices. Studies show that coaching is particularly effective in helping teachers make significant changes in their instructional methods (Kraft, Blazar, & Hogan, 2018).

IMPLEMENTING EVIDENCE-BASED TEACHING PRACTICES

Evidence-based teaching practices are instructional methods and strategies that have been proven effective through rigorous research and evaluation. Implementing these practices can lead to improved student learning and achievement.

IDENTIFYING EFFECTIVE PRACTICES

The process of identifying and implementing evidence-based practices involves reviewing educational research, analyzing data, and continuously evaluating the impact of instructional methods on student outcomes. Resources such as the What Works Clearinghouse (WWC) provide educators with access to research-based recommendations and evidence ratings for various teaching practices.

> Examples of Evidence-Based Practices

1. **Active Learning**: Active learning strategies, such as collaborative group work, problem-based learning, and interactive discussions, engage students in the learning process and promote deeper understanding. Research by Freeman et al. (2014) found that active learning significantly increases student performance in science, engineering, and mathematics courses.
2. **Formative Assessment**: Formative assessment involves using ongoing assessments to monitor student progress and provide feedback that guides instructional decisions. Studies by Black and Wiliam (1998) demonstrate that formative assessment can lead to substantial gains in student achievement, particularly when used to inform teaching practices.
3. **Differentiated Instruction**: Differentiated instruction tailors teaching methods and materials to meet the diverse needs of students. This approach is supported by research indicating that differentiation can enhance student engagement and achievement by providing appropriate challenges and supports for all learners (Tomlinson, 2001).

> Supporting Educators in Implementing Evidence-Based Practices

1. **Access to Resources**: Providing educators with access to high-quality resources and research-based materials is crucial for the successful implementation of evidence-based practices. Schools should invest in educational databases, professional development libraries, and online platforms that offer instructional guides and best practices.
2. **Collaborative Planning Time**: Allocating time for teachers to collaborate and plan together is essential for integrating evidence-based practices into their instruction. Collaborative planning allows teachers to share insights, develop cohesive strategies, and support each other in implementing new methods.
3. **Ongoing Evaluation and Feedback**: Continuous evaluation and feedback help teachers refine their practices and ensure that they are effectively meeting students' needs. Schools should establish systems for regular classroom observations, peer reviews, and student feedback to inform instructional improvements.

Mobilizing educators and school leaders through professional development and continuous learning is vital for fostering high-quality education. By prioritizing ongoing professional growth and implementing evidence-based teaching practices, educators can enhance their instructional effectiveness and improve student outcomes. This call to action urges educators, parents, and policymakers to invest in professional development, support collaborative learning environments, and commit to evidence-based education. Together, these efforts will ensure that students receive the best possible education and are prepared to thrive in a rapidly changing world.

> # Engaging Parents and Policymakers

ADVOCATING FOR POLICY CHANGES THAT SUPPORT INNOVATIVE EDUCATION

To create a transformative educational system that prepares students for the complexities of the modern world, it is essential to advocate for policy changes that support innovative education. Policymakers play a crucial role in shaping the educational landscape by enacting legislation and allocating resources that can foster progressive teaching practices and inclusive learning environments.

THE NEED FOR POLICY REFORM

Educational policies must evolve to address the current and future needs of students. Traditional education models, often focused on rote memorization and standardized testing, do not adequately prepare students for the dynamic and interconnected global economy. Instead, there is a need for policies that promote critical thinking, creativity, digital literacy, and lifelong learning.

Research by Darling-Hammond et al. (2019) highlights the importance of adopting 21st-century skills frameworks, which emphasize competencies such as problem-solving, collaboration, and digital literacy. These frameworks should be embedded in national and state education standards to ensure that all students receive a relevant and forward-thinking education.

Examples of Innovative Education Policies

1. **Personalized Learning Initiatives**: Personalized learning tailors education to individual students' strengths, needs, and interests. Policies supporting personalized learning can include funding for adaptive learning technologies, professional development for teachers on personalized instruction, and flexible curriculum guidelines. A study by Pane et al. (2017) found that personalized learning approaches can significantly improve student achievement, particularly in reading and math.
2. **STEM and STEAM Education**: Promoting STEM (Science, Technology, Engineering, and Mathematics) and STEAM (adding Arts) education is crucial for preparing students for future careers. Policies that fund STEM/STEAM programs, provide grants for schools to develop innovative STEM curricula, and support partnerships between schools and technology companies can enhance students' skills and interest in these fields. The National Science Foundation (2019) reports that STEM education initiatives have led to increased student engagement and higher academic performance in STEM subjects.
3. **Early Childhood Education**: Investing in early childhood education is critical for long-term academic and social success. Policies that expand access to high-quality pre-kindergarten programs, provide resources for early childhood educators, and emphasize the importance of play-based learning can have lasting positive effects. Research by Heckman (2011) demonstrates that early childhood education significantly improves outcomes in education, health, and economic productivity.

CREATING A SUPPORTIVE NETWORK FOR EDUCATIONAL INITIATIVES

Building a supportive network for educational initiatives involves engaging various stakeholders, including parents, educators, community leaders, and policymakers. Collaborative efforts can drive meaningful change and ensure that educational innovations are effectively implemented and sustained.

PARENTAL ENGAGEMENT

Parents play a vital role in supporting their children's education. Schools can engage parents by involving them in decision-making processes, offering workshops on how to support learning at home, and creating volunteer opportunities. According to Henderson and Mapp (2002), strong home-school partnerships lead to higher student achievement, better attendance, and improved behavior.

> Strategies for Engaging Parents

1. **Regular Communication**: Establishing clear and consistent communication channels between schools and parents helps build trust and keeps parents informed about their children's progress and school activities. Schools can use newsletters, emails, social media, and parent-teacher conferences to maintain open lines of communication.
2. **Parent Education Programs**: Offering workshops and resources on topics such as literacy development, digital safety, and college readiness can empower parents to support their children's education more effectively. These programs can

also address specific needs, such as language support for non-English-speaking families.
3. **Volunteer Opportunities**: Encouraging parents to volunteer in classrooms, school events, and extracurricular activities fosters a sense of community and involvement. Schools can create diverse volunteer opportunities that cater to different interests and schedules.

POLICYMAKER ENGAGEMENT

Engaging policymakers is crucial for advocating for education reform and securing necessary funding and resources. Schools and educational organizations can work together to raise awareness about the importance of innovative education policies and the impact of these policies on student outcomes.

> Strategies for Engaging Policymakers

1. **Building Relationships**: Establishing relationships with local, state, and federal policymakers can help create advocates for education reform. Schools can invite policymakers to visit classrooms, attend school events, and meet with educators, students, and parents to understand the challenges and successes of the education system.
2. **Data-Driven Advocacy**: Using data and research to highlight the effectiveness of innovative educational practices can strengthen the case for policy changes. Schools can share success stories, student performance data, and research findings with policymakers to demonstrate the impact of proposed reforms.
3. **Collaborative Coalitions**: Forming coalitions with other

schools, educational organizations, and community groups can amplify advocacy efforts. These coalitions can organize campaigns, public forums, and meetings with policymakers to discuss education priorities and advocate for necessary changes.

Engaging parents and policymakers is essential for advocating for policy changes that support innovative education and creating a supportive network for educational initiatives. By involving parents in their children's education and building strong relationships with policymakers, schools can drive meaningful reform and ensure that all students receive a high-quality, forward-thinking education. These collaborative efforts will help create an education system that prepares students to thrive in the 21st century and contribute to a brighter, more equitable world.

11

Conclusion: The Everlasting Light of Knowledge and Service

Recap of the Key Themes and Messages of the Book

The Transformative Power of Education

EDUCATION AS A PATH FROM IGNORANCE TO ENLIGHTENMENT

Throughout this book, we have explored the profound impact of education as a means to dispel darkness and bring forth the light of knowledge. Education is not merely the acquisition of facts and figures; it is the journey from ignorance to enlightenment, where individuals learn to think critically, question assumptions, and seek deeper understanding. As Jesus said on the cross, "Forgive them, for they know not what they do" (Luke 23:34, NIV), highlighting that ignorance often underpins misguided actions. Education shines a light on ignorance, revealing pathways to wisdom and compassion.

This transformative power of education is evident in its ability to change lives and uplift communities. It equips individuals with the skills and knowledge necessary to navigate the complexities of the modern world. From ancient philosophers like Socrates, who believed that an unexamined life is not worth living, to contemporary educators advocating for lifelong learning, the essence of education remains the same: to illuminate minds and hearts, enabling people to see the world with clarity and purpose.

THE ROLE OF HOLISTIC AND INCLUSIVE EDUCATION IN SHAPING FUTURE LEADERS

Holistic and inclusive education is essential for developing well-rounded individuals who are not only intellectually competent but also emotionally and socially aware. This approach recognizes that true education goes beyond academic achievements; it nurtures the whole person, fostering empathy, resilience, and a sense of responsibility towards others.

Holistic education integrates various dimensions of learning, including emotional, social, physical, and spiritual development. It encourages students to connect with their inner selves and the world around them, promoting a balanced and fulfilling life. As noted by Miller (2000), holistic education helps students develop a sense of purpose and interconnectedness, which is crucial for personal and societal well-being.

Inclusive education ensures that all students, regardless of their backgrounds or abilities, have access to high-quality learning opportunities. It emphasizes equity and fairness, providing support and resources to those who need them most. Inclusive education not only benefits individuals but also strengthens communities by fostering mutual respect and understanding. According to UNESCO (2016), inclusive education promotes social cohesion and reduces discrimination, leading to better educational and social outcomes for all students.

SHAPING FUTURE LEADERS

The leaders of tomorrow are being shaped in the classrooms of today. By emphasizing holistic and inclusive education, we are preparing future leaders who are capable of addressing the multifaceted challenges of our world. These leaders will be critical thinkers, compassionate individuals, and proactive change-makers, equipped to make informed decisions and drive positive social impact.

Programs that integrate leadership development, service learning, and community engagement help students develop the skills and values necessary for effective leadership. For instance, the incorporation of project-based learning and real-world applications at AA STEAM & Entrepreneurship Academy ensures that students are not only academically proficient but also prepared to lead with integrity and vision.

Research supports the effectiveness of these educational approaches. A study by Darling-Hammond et al. (2019) emphasizes that students who experience holistic and inclusive education demonstrate higher levels of academic achievement, social skills, and overall well-being. These students are better equipped to navigate the complexities of the modern world and to lead with empathy and resilience.

Education, in its truest sense, is the pathway from ignorance to enlightenment. By embracing holistic and inclusive education, we can shape future leaders who are not only knowledgeable but also empathetic and socially responsible. The transformative power of education lies in its ability to illuminate minds and hearts, fostering a generation of individuals prepared to contribute to a brighter, more equitable world. As we continue this journey of light and knowledge, let us commit to nurturing the potential within every student, ensuring that they are equipped to lead with wisdom and compassion.

Reflecting on my journey as an educator and spiritual seeker, I am filled with gratitude for the experiences and lessons that have shaped my vision for education and society. This journey has reinforced my belief in the transformative power of education and the importance of fostering a holistic, inclusive, and compassionate approach to learning. As we move forward, I am committed to continuing this journey of light and knowledge, striving to create an educational environment that empowers every student to reach their full potential and contribute to a brighter, more equitable world. Through education and service, we can illuminate the path from ignorance to enlightenment, guiding future generations toward wisdom, compassion, and positive change.

References

References

Abrami, P. C., Bernard, R. M., Borokhovski, E., Wade, A., Surkes, M. A., Tamim, R., & Zhang, D. (2015). Strategies for Teaching Students to Think Critically: A Meta-Analysis. *Review of Educational Research, 85*(2), 275-314.

Ali, S. R., & Gibbs, J. T. (1998). A Faith-based Approach to Academic Achievement in African American Students. *Journal of Negro Education, 67*(1), 4-20.

Allport, G. W. (1954). *The Nature of Prejudice*. Addison-Wesley.

American Psychological Association (APA). (2019). Effects of Poverty, Hunger, and Homelessness on Children and Youth. Retrieved from https://www.apa.org/pi/families/poverty

Angrist, J. D., Pathak, P. A., & Walters, C. R. (2013). Explaining Charter School Effectiveness. *American Economic Journal: Applied Economics*.

Armstrong, K. (1993). *A History of God: The 4,000-Year Quest of Judaism, Christianity, and Islam*. Knopf.

Astin, A. W., & Sax, L. J. (1998). How Undergraduates are Affected by Service Participation. *Journal of College Student Development, 39*(3), 251-263.

Astin, A. W., Vogelgesang, L. J., Ikeda, E. K., & Yee, J. A.

(2000). *How Service Learning Affects Students*. Higher Education Research Institute, University of California, Los Angeles.

Axtell, J. (1968). *The Educational Writings of John Locke*. Cambridge University Press.

Baines, J., & Yoffee, N. (1998). *Order, Legitimacy, and Wealth in Ancient States*. Cambridge University Press.

Banks, J. A. (2008). *Diversity and Citizenship Education: Global Perspectives*. Jossey-Bass.

Banks, J. A. (2015). *Cultural Diversity and Education*. Routledge.

Bandura, A. (2001). Social Cognitive Theory: An Agentic Perspective. *Annual Review of Psychology, 52*, 1-26.

Battistich, V., Solomon, D., Watson, M., & Schaps, E. (1997). Caring School Communities. *Educational Psychologist, 32*(3), 137-151.

Bell, S. (2010). Project-Based Learning for the 21st Century: Skills for the Future. *The Clearing House: A Journal of Educational Strategies, Issues and Ideas, 83*(2), 39-43.

Berkowitz, M. W., & Bier, M. C. (2005). What Works in Character Education: A Research-Driven Guide for Educators. *Character Education Partnership*.

Billig, S. H. (2000). Research on K-12 School-Based Service-Learning: The Evidence Builds. *Phi Delta Kappan, 81*(9), 658-664.

Blake, M., Lee, S., & DeGraw, T. (2020). One for One: The Impact of Social Entrepreneurship on Global Health. *Social Enterprise Journal, 16*(3), 235-250.

Blakely, S. (2019). *The Spanx Story: What You Didn't Know About the Woman Behind the Billion-Dollar Brand*. Wiley.

Blomberg, C. L. (2012). *Interpreting the Parables*. InterVarsity Press.

Boaler, J. (1999). Mathematics for the Moment, or the Millennium? Education Week. *Teaching for Meaningful Understanding: A Review of Research on Inquiry-Based and Cooperative Learning*.

Boston Public Schools. (2019). *Biotech in Boston Public Schools*. Retrieved from https://www.bostonpublicschools.org/Page/6580

Bosma, N., Hill, S., Ionescu-Somers, A., Guerrero, M., Kelley, D., Levie, J., & Tarnawa, A. (2021). *Global Entrepreneurship Monitor 2020/2021 Global Report*. Global Entrepreneurship Research Association.

Botvin, G. J., & Griffin, K. W. (2004). Life Skills Training: Empirical Findings and Future Directions. *The Journal of Primary Prevention, 25*(2), 211-232.

Bovens, M. (2007). Analyzing and Assessing Accountability: A Conceptual Framework. *European Law Journal, 13*(4), 447-468.

Boyd, W. (1956). *Emile for Today: The Emile of Jean Jacques Rousseau*. Greenwood Press.

Brickhouse, T. C., & Smith, N. D. (1994). *Plato's Socrates*. Oxford University Press.

Bridges, R. (1999). *Through My Eyes*. Scholastic Press.

Brown, T. (2009). *Change by Design: How Design Thinking Transforms Organizations and Inspires Innovation*. Harper Business.

Bryson, J. M., Crosby, B. C., & Stone, M. M. (2015). Designing and Implementing Cross-Sector Collaborations: Needed and Challenging. *Public Administration Review, 75*(5), 647-663.

Buck Institute for Education. (2018). *Project-Based Learning Research Summary: Studies Validate PBL Benefits*. Retrieved from https://www.pblworks.org/research

Cardus Education Survey. (2018). *Cardus Education Survey: 2018 Report*. Retrieved from https://www.cardus.ca/research/education/reports/cardus-education-survey-2018/

Carson, B. (1992). *Gifted Hands: The Ben Carson Story*. Zondervan.

CAST. (2018). *Universal Design for Learning Guidelines Version 2.2*. Retrieved from http://udlguidelines.cast.org

Center for Information & Research on Civic Learning and Engagement (CIRCLE). (2013). *All Together Now: Collaboration and Innovation for Youth Engagement*. Retrieved from https://circle.tufts.edu/latest-research/all-together-now-collaboration-and-innovation-youth-engagement

Cochran-Smith, M. (2004). *Walking the Road: Race, Diversity, and Social Justice in Teacher Education*. Teachers College Press.

Coles, R. (1995). *The Story of Ruby Bridges*. Scholastic.

Conley, D. T., & Ward, T. (2009). *International Baccalaureate Standards Development and Alignment Project*. Educational Policy Improvement Center.

Cremin, L. A. (1957). *The Republic and the School: Horace Mann on the Education of Free Men*. Teachers College Press.

Darling-Hammond, L., Barron, B., Pearson, P. D., Schoenfeld, A. H., Stage, E. K., Zimmerman, T. D., ... & Tilson, J. L. (2008). *Powerful Learning: What We Know About Teaching for Understanding*. John Wiley & Sons.

Darling-Hammond, L., Flook, L., Cook-Harvey, C., Barron, B., & Osher, D. (2019). Implications for Educational Practice of the Science of Learning and Development. *Applied Developmental Science*, 24(2), 97-140.

Darling-Hammond, L., Hyler, M. E., & Gardner, M. (2017). *Effective Teacher Professional Development*. Learning Policy Institute.

Deci, E. L., & Ryan, R. M. (2000). The "What" and "Why" of Goal Pursuits: Human Needs and the Self-Determination of Behavior. *Psychological Inquiry*, 11(4), 227-268.

De Haan, J., Elfers, H., & Reitsma, J. (2012). Junior Achievement's Impact on Financial Literacy and Entrepreneurship. *Journal of Economic Education*, 43(3), 260-272.

Dewey, J. (1938). *Experience and Education*. Kappa Delta Pi.

Dobbie, W., & Fryer, R. G. (2011). Are High-Quality Schools Enough to Increase Achievement Among the Poor? Evidence from the Harlem Children's Zone. *American Economic Journal: Applied Economics*.

Doran, A. (2005). *Tikkun Olam: Social Responsibility in Jewish Thought and Law*. JPS.

Dovidio, J. F., Glick, P., & Rudman, L. A. (2010). *On the Nature of Prejudice: Fifty Years after Allport*. Wiley-Blackwell.

Dugan, J. P., & Komives, S. R. (2007). Developing Leadership Capacity in College Students: Findings from a National Study. *National Clearinghouse for Leadership Programs*.

Duckworth, A. L., Peterson, C., Matthews, M. D., & Kelly, D. R. (2007). Grit: Perseverance and Passion for Long-Term Goals. *Journal of Personality and Social Psychology, 92*(6), 1087-1101.

Durlak, J. A., Weissberg, R. P., Dymnicki, A. B., Taylor, R. D., & Schellinger, K. B. (2011). The Impact of Enhancing Students' Social and Emotional Learning: A Meta-Analysis of School-Based Universal Interventions. *Child Development, 82*(1), 405-432.

Dyer, J. H., Gregersen, H. B., & Christensen, C. M. (2011). *The Innovator's DNA: Mastering the Five Skills of Disruptive Innovators*. Harvard Business Review Press.

Easton, F. (1997). Educating the Whole Child, "Head, Heart, and Hands": Learning from the Waldorf Experience. *Theory Into Practice, 36*(2), 87-94.

Education Trust. (2018). *Funding Gaps 2018: An Analysis of School Funding Equity Across the U.S. and Within Each State*. Retrieved from https://edtrust.org/resource/funding-gaps-2018/

Elman, B. A. (2000). *A Cultural History of Civil Examinations in Late Imperial China*. University of California Press.

Epstein, J. L. (2011). *School, Family, and Community Partnerships: Preparing Educators and Improving Schools*. Westview Press.

Esposito, J. L. (2002). *What Everyone Needs to Know About Islam*. Oxford University Press.

European Commission. (2013). *Entrepreneurship Education: A Guide for Educators*. Retrieved from https://ec.europa.eu/docsroom/documents/7465/attachments/1/translations/en/renditions/native

Eyler, J., & Giles, D. E. (1999). *Where's the Learning in Service-Learning?* Jossey-Bass.

Eyler, J., Giles, D. E., & Schmiede, A. (1996). *A Practitioner's Guide to Reflection in Service-Learning: Student Voices and Reflections*. Vanderbilt University.

Fenske, R. H., Geranios, C. A., Keller, J. E., & Moore, D. E. (2000). Early Intervention Programs: Opening the Door to Higher Education. *ASHE-ERIC Higher Education Report, 25*(6), 1-119.

Freeman, S., Eddy, S. L., McDonough, M., Smith, M. K., Okoroafor, N., Jordt, H., & Wenderoth, M. P. (2014). Active Learning Increases Student Performance in Science, Engineering, and Mathematics. *Proceedings of the National Academy of Sciences, 111*(23), 8410-8415.

Freire, P. (1970). *Pedagogy of the Oppressed*. Continuum.

Fraser, W. J. (2014). *The Development of Compulsory Education in Prussia*. Routledge.

Garces, E., Thomas, D., & Currie, J. (2002). Longer-Term Effects of Head Start. *American Economic Review, 92*(4), 999-1012.

Gates, B. (2018). M-KOPA Solar: Harnessing the Power of the Sun to Transform Lives. *Gates Notes*.

Gay, G. (2010). *Culturally Responsive Teaching: Theory, Research, and Practice*. Teachers College Press.

Gay, P. (1964). *The Enlightenment: An Interpretation*. Alfred A. Knopf.

Goleman, D. (1995). *Emotional Intelligence: Why It Can Matter More Than IQ*. Bantam Books.

Greenberg, M. T., Weissberg, R. P., O'Brien, M. U., Zins, J. E., Fredericks, L., Resnik, H., & Elias, M. J. (2003). Enhancing School-Based Prevention and Youth Development through Coordinated Social, Emotional, and Academic Learning. *American Psychologist, 58*(6-7), 466-474.

Greenleaf, R. K. (1977). *Servant Leadership: A Journey into the Nature of Legitimate Power and Greatness*. Paulist Press.

Guo, J. J., Jang, R., Keller, K. N., McCracken, A. L., Pan, W.,

& Cluxton, R. J. (2008). Impact of School-Based Health Centers on Students with Mental Health Problems. *Public Health Reports, 123*(6), 768-780.

Heckman, J. J. (2011). The Economics of Inequality: The Value of Early Childhood Education. *American Educator, 35*(1), 31-35.

Henderson, A. T., & Mapp, K. L. (2002). *A New Wave of Evidence: The Impact of School, Family, and Community Connections on Student Achievement*. National Center for Family & Community Connections with Schools.

Hill, J. P., & Den Dulk, K. R. (2013). Religion, Volunteering, and Educational Setting: The Effect of Youth Schooling Type on Civic Engagement. *Journal for the Scientific Study of Religion, 52*(1), 179-197.

hooks, b. (1994). *Teaching to Transgress: Education as the Practice of Freedom*. Routledge.

Hrabowski, F. A. (2012). *Holding Fast to Dreams: Empowering Youth from the Civil Rights Crusade to STEM Achievement*. Beacon Press.

IBM. (2020). *P-TECH: Pathways in Technology Early College High Schools*. Retrieved from https://www.ibm.com/impact/initiatives/education/ptech

Institute for the Future. (2011). *Future Work Skills 2020*. Retrieved from http://www.iftf.org/uploads/media/SR-1382A_UPRI_future_work_skills_sm.pdf

International Renewable Energy Agency (IRENA). (2013). *Renewable Energy and Jobs*. Retrieved from https://www.irena.org/publications/2013/Dec/Renewable-Energy-and-Jobs

International Society for Technology in Education (ISTE). (2016). *ISTE Standards for Students*. Retrieved from https://www.iste.org/standards/for-students

Jaeger, W. (1943). *Paideia: The Ideals of Greek Culture*. Oxford University Press.

Jacobs, H. H. (1989). *Interdisciplinary Curriculum: Design and Implementation*. ASCD.

Jeynes, W. H. (2012). A Meta-Analysis on the Effects and Contributions of Public, Public Charter, and Religious Schools on Student Outcomes. *Peabody Journal of Education, 87*(3), 305-335.

Johnson, D. W., & Johnson, R. T. (1989). *Cooperation and Competition: Theory and Research*. Interaction Book Company.

Johnson, D. W., & Johnson, R. T. (2009). An Educational Psychology Success Story: Social Interdependence Theory and Cooperative Learning. *Educational Researcher, 38*(5), 365-379.

Kaplan, M., & Hanhardt, A. (2003). Intergenerational Programs in Schools: Considerations of Form and Function. *International Journal of Aging and Human Development, 57*(1), 1-25.

Kelley, K. (2010). *Oprah: A Biography*. Crown Archetype.

Khandker, S. R., & Samad, H. A. (2014). Dynamic Effects of Microcredit in Bangladesh. *World Bank Policy Research Working Paper No. 6821*.

Khantzian, E. J. (2017). The Self-Medication Hypothesis of Substance Use Disorders: A Reconsideration and Recent Applications. *Harvard Review of Psychiatry, 25*(5), 231-244.

Kluger, R. (1975). *Simple Justice: The History of Brown v. Board of Education and Black America's Struggle for Equality*. Knopf.

Kolb, D. A. (1984). *Experiential Learning: Experience as the Source of Learning and Development*. Prentice-Hall.

Koob, G. F., & Volkow, N. D. (2016). Neurobiology of Addiction: A Neurocircuitry Analysis. *The Lancet Psychiatry, 3*(8), 760-773.

Kopp, W. (2011). *A Chance to Make History: What Works and What Doesn't in Providing an Excellent Education for All*. PublicAffairs.

Krajcik, J. S., & Blumenfeld, P. C. (2006). Project-Based Learning. In R. K. Sawyer (Ed.), *The Cambridge Handbook of the Learning Sciences* (pp. 317-333). Cambridge University Press.

Kraft, M. A., Blazar, D., & Hogan, D. (2018). The Effect of Teacher Coaching on Instruction and Achievement: A Meta-Analysis of the Causal Evidence. *Review of Educational Research, 88*(4), 547-588.

Laudet, A. B., Magura, S., Vogel, H. S., & Knight, E. L. (2007). Perceived Social Support and Recovery Status: The Role of Lifestyle Factors among Persons in Recovery from Substance Use Disorders. *Substance Use & Misuse, 42*(2-3), 95-113.

Luckin, R., Holmes, W., Griffiths, M., & Forcier, L. B. (2016). *Intelligence Unleashed: An Argument for AI in Education*. Pearson.

Lusardi, A., & Mitchell, O. S. (2014). The Economic Importance of Financial Literacy: Theory and Evidence. *Journal of Economic Literature, 52*(1), 5-44.

Loyola University Chicago. (2020). *Alumni Impact Report*. Retrieved from https://www.luc.edu/alumni/impactreport2020/

Mandela, N. (1994). *Long Walk to Freedom: The Autobiography of Nelson Mandela*. Little, Brown and Company.

Mandela, N. (2003). Education is the Most Powerful Weapon. Retrieved from Nelson Mandela Foundation.

Mandell, L., & Klein, L. S. (2009). The Impact of Financial Literacy Education on Subsequent Financial Behavior. *Journal of Financial Counseling and Planning, 20*(1), 15-24.

Markus, G. B., Howard, J. P. F., & King, D. C. (1993). Integrating Community Service and Classroom Instruction Enhances Learning: Results from an Experiment. *Educational Evaluation and Policy Analysis, 15*(4), 410-419.

McGrath, A. E. (2006). *Christian Theology: An Introduction*. Blackwell Publishing.

Means, B., Toyama, Y., Murphy, R., Bakia, M., & Jones, K. (2013). The Effectiveness of Online and Blended Learning: A Meta-Analysis of the Empirical Literature. *Teachers College Record*.

Miller, J. P. (2000). *Education and the Soul: Toward a Spiritual Curriculum*. SUNY Press.

Miller, R. (2000). *Caring for New Life: Essays on Holistic Education*. Foundation for Educational Renewal.

Miyazaki, I. (1976). *China's Examination Hell: The Civil Service Examinations of Imperial China*. Yale University Press.

Molnar, A. R. (1997). Computers in Education: A Brief History. *The Journal*.

Morduch, J. (1999). The Microfinance Promise. *Journal of Economic Literature*, 37(4), 1569-1614.

Morelli, S. A., Rameson, L. T., & Lieberman, M. D. (2015). The Neural Components of Empathy: Predicting Daily Prosocial Behavior. *Social Cognitive and Affective Neuroscience*, 9(1), 39-47.

Morris, M. H., Kuratko, D. F., & Cornwall, J. R. (2013). *Entrepreneurship Programs and the Modern University*. Edward Elgar Publishing.

Muller, C., & Ellison, C. G. (2001). Religious Involvement, Social Capital, and Adolescents' Academic Progress: Evidence from the National Longitudinal Study of Adolescent Health. *Sociological Focus*, 34(2), 155-183.

Mundaka Upanishad. (n.d.). *The Upanishads*.

Murphy, S. E., & Johnson, S. K. (2011). The Benefits of a Long-Lens Approach to Leader Development: Understanding the Seeds of Leadership. *The Leadership Quarterly*, 22(3), 459-470.

Myers, D., & Schirm, A. (1999). The Impacts of Upward Bound: Final Report for Phase I of the National Evaluation. *Mathematica Policy Research, Inc.*.

National Association of Secondary School Principals (NASSP). (2016). *Making the Case for Business-Education Partnerships*. Retrieved from https://www.nassp.org/Content.aspx?topic=Making_the_Case_for_Business_Education_Partnerships

National Center for Education Statistics (NCES). (2016). *Private School Universe Survey, 2013-14*. U.S. Department of Education.

National Financial Educators Council (NFEC). (2020). *Financial Literacy Definition*. Retrieved from https://www.financialeducatorscouncil.org/financial-literacy-definition

National Institute on Drug Abuse (NIDA). (2018). Genetics and Epigenetics of Addiction. Retrieved from https://www.drugabuse.gov/publications/drugfacts/genetics-epigenetics-addiction

National Institute on Drug Abuse (NIDA). (2020). Understanding Drug Use and Addiction. Retrieved from https://www.drugabuse.gov/publications/drugfacts/understanding-drug-use-addiction

National Science Foundation. (2019). *STEM Education and Workforce*. Retrieved from https://www.nsf.gov/edu/

Neck, H. M., Greene, P. G., & Brush, C. G. (2014). *Teaching Entrepreneurship: A Practice-Based Approach*. Edward Elgar Publishing.

Nucci, L. P., & Narvaez, D. (2008). *Handbook of Moral and Character Education*. Routledge.

Nussbaum, M. C. (2010). *Not for Profit: Why Democracy Needs the Humanities*. Princeton University Press.

Obama, M. (2018). *Becoming*. Crown Publishing Group.

OECD. (2014). *PISA 2012 Results: Creative Problem Solving: Students' Skills in Tackling Real-Life Problems (Volume V)*. OECD Publishing.

OECD. (2017). *Enhancing the Contributions of SMEs in a Global and Digitalised Economy*. Meeting of the OECD Council at Ministerial Level. Paris, France.

OECD. (2019). *Trends Shaping Education 2019*. OECD Publishing. Retrieved from https://www.oecd.org/education/trends-shaping-education-22187049.htm

Oprah Winfrey Leadership Academy Foundation. (2021). *Our Mission and History*. Retrieved from https://www.owla.org/

Oppenheim, A. L. (1964). *Ancient Mesopotamia: Portrait of a Dead Civilization*. University of Chicago Press.

Patel, E., & Meyer, C. (2011). The Role of Interfaith Dialogue in Building Relationships and Respect Among Students. *Journal of College and Character, 12*(1), 1-9.

Pappano, L. (2012). The Year of the MOOC. *The New York Times*.

Pane, J. F., Steiner, E. D., Baird, M. D., Hamilton, L. S., & Pane, J. D. (2017). Informing Progress: Insights on Personalized Learning Implementation and Effects. *RAND Corporation*.

Partnership for 21st Century Skills. (2010). *21st Century Skills, Education & Competitiveness: A Resource and Policy Guide*. Retrieved from http://www.p21.org/storage/documents/21st_century_skills_education_and_competitiveness_guide.pdf

Patel, E., & Meyer, C. (2011). The Role of Interfaith Dialogue in Building Relationships and Respect Among Students. *Journal of College and Character*, 12(1), 1-9.

Posner, J. (2010). Shining Hope for Communities: Bridging the Gap. *SHOFCO Annual Report*.

Prothero, S. (2010). *God Is Not One: The Eight Rival Religions That Run the World*. HarperOne.

Rahula, W. (1959). *What the Buddha Taught*. Grove Press.

Radhakrishnan, S. (1953). *The Principal Upanishads*. HarperCollins.

Regnerus, M. D., & Elder, G. H. (2003). Religion and Vulnerability Among Low-Risk Adolescents. *Social Science Research*, 32(4), 633-658.

Robins, G. (1993). *Women in Ancient Egypt*. Harvard University Press.

Rockefeller Foundation. (2014). *Digital Jobs: Building Skills for the Future*. Retrieved from https://www.rockefellerfoundation.org/report/digital-jobs-building-skills-future/

Room to Read. (2019). *Annual Report 2019*. Retrieved from https://www.roomtoread.org

Sahlberg, P. (2011). *Finnish Lessons: What Can the World Learn from Educational Change in Finland?* Teachers College Press.

Said, C. (2013). Google Executives Support Montessori Education. *San Francisco Chronicle*. Retrieved from https://www.sfgate.com/business/article/Google-executives-support-Montessori-education-4440369.php

Sanergy. (2017). *Sanergy Annual Report 2017*. Retrieved from https://www.sanergy.com/annual-report-2017

Scales, P. C., Blyth, D. A., Berkas, T. H., & Kielsmeier, J. C. (2000). The Effects of Service-Learning on Middle School Students' Social Responsibility and Academic Success. *Journal of Early Adolescence, 20*(3), 332-358.

Seligman, M. E. P., & Csikszentmihalyi, M. (2000). Positive Psychology: An Introduction. *American Psychologist, 55*(1), 5-14.

Sheff, D. (2008). *Beautiful Boy: A Father's Journey Through His Son's Addiction*. Houghton Mifflin Harcourt.

Sheff, N. (2009). *Tweak: Growing Up on Methamphetamines*. Atheneum Books for Young Readers.

Simons, T. (2002). The High Cost of Lost Trust. *Harvard Business Review, 80*(9), 18-19.

Slavin, R. E., Madden, N. A., Chambers, B., & Haxby, B. (2009). *Two Million Children: Success for All*. Corwin Press.

Smith, C., & Denton, M. L. (2005). *Soul Searching: The Religious and Spiritual Lives of American Teenagers*. Oxford University Press.

Smith, C., & Snell, P. (2009). *Souls in Transition: The Religious and Spiritual Lives of Emerging Adults*. Oxford University Press.

Smithson, M. (2008). *Ignorance and Uncertainty: Emerging Paradigms*. Springer.

Sotomayor, S. (2013). *My Beloved World*. Knopf.

Stevenson, B. (2015). Building Bridges: The Impact of Service Learning on Cultural Competence. *Amigos de las Américas Alumni Reflections*.

Stern, J. (2004). Interfaith Education: A Conceptual and Practical Framework. *Religious Education, 99*(1), 5-20.

Sternberg, R. J. (2001). *Wisdom, Intelligence, and Creativity Synthesized*. Cambridge University Press.

Substance Abuse and Mental Health Services Administration (SAMHSA). (2020). *Key Substance Use and Mental Health Indicators in the United States: Results from the 2019 National Survey on Drug Use and Health*. Retrieved from https://www.samhsa.gov/data/report/2019-nsduh-annual-national-report

Sugai, G., & Horner, R. H. (2002). The Evolution of Discipline Practices: School-Wide Positive Behavior Supports. *Child & Family Behavior Therapy*, 24(1-2), 23-50.

Telushkin, J. (1991). *Jewish Literacy: The Most Important Things to Know About the Jewish Religion, Its People, and Its History*. William Morrow.

Tent Partnership for Refugees. (2019). *Tent Annual Report 2019*. Retrieved from https://www.tent.org/annual-report-2019

The Holy Bible, New International Version. (2011). Luke 23:34. Biblica, Inc.

The Holy Bible, New International Version. (2011). Galatians 5:13. Biblica, Inc.

The Ursuline School. (2021). *Habitat for Humanity Project Summary*. Retrieved from https://www.ursuline.edu/habitat-project-2021

Tomlinson, C. A. (2001). *How to Differentiate Instruction in Mixed-Ability Classrooms*. ASCD.

Topping, K. J. (2005). Trends in Peer Learning. *Educational Psychology*, 25(6), 631-645.

Tough, P. (2008). *Whatever It Takes: Geoffrey Canada's Quest to Change Harlem and America*. Houghton Mifflin Harcourt.

Tracy, K., & Wallace, S. P. (2016). Benefits of Peer Support Groups in the Treatment of Addiction. *Substance Use & Misuse*, 51(2), 202-212.

UNESCO. (2014). *Education for Sustainable Development Goals: Learning Objectives*. United Nations Educational, Scientific and Cultural Organization.

UNESCO. (2014). *Shaping the Future We Want: UN Decade of*

Education for Sustainable Development (2005-2014) Final Report. United Nations Educational, Scientific and Cultural Organization. Retrieved from https://unesdoc.unesco.org/ark:/48223/pf0000230171

UNESCO. (2015). *Education 2030: Incheon Declaration and Framework for Action*. Retrieved from https://unesdoc.unesco.org/ark:/48223/pf0000233291

UNESCO. (2016). *Leaving No One Behind: The Imperative of Inclusive Development. Report on the World Social Situation 2016*. Retrieved from https://www.un.org/esa/socdev/rwss/2016/full-report.pdf

UNESCO. (2015). *Teaching and Learning: Achieving Quality for All*. Retrieved from https://unesdoc.unesco.org/ark:/48223/pf0000237451

UNESCO. (2015). *Global Citizenship Education: Topics and Learning Objectives*. United Nations Educational, Scientific and Cultural Organization. Retrieved from https://unesdoc.unesco.org/ark:/48223/pf0000233291

United Nations. (2016). *Leaving No One Behind: The Imperative of Inclusive Development. Report on the World Social Situation 2016*. Retrieved from https://www.un.org/esa/socdev/rwss/2016/full-report.pdf

USDOE. (2016). *STEM 2026: A Vision for Innovation in STEM Education*. U.S. Department of Education.

Van De Mieroop, M. (1999). *Cuneiform Texts and the Writing of History*. Routledge.

Vance, A. (2015). *Elon Musk: Tesla, SpaceX, and the Quest for a Fantastic Future*. Ecco.

Vickers, B. (1992). Francis Bacon and the Progress of Knowledge. *Journal of the History of Ideas, 53*(3), 495-518.

Villegas, A. M., & Lucas, T. (2002). *Educating Culturally Responsive Teachers: A Coherent Approach*. SUNY Press.

Ware, S. (1981). *Beyond Suffrage: Women in the New Deal*. Harvard University Press.

Watson, D. C., Milliron, V., & Morris, P. (2013). Faith-Based

Education and the Academic and Personal Development of Students. *Journal of Research on Christian Education, 22*(2), 173-193.

Wells, N. M., & Lekies, K. S. (2006). Nature and the Life Course: Pathways from Childhood Nature Experiences to Adult Environmentalism. *Children, Youth and Environments, 16*(1), 1-24.

Wilkins, M. J. (1992). *Following the Master: Discipleship in the Steps of Jesus*. Zondervan.

World Bank. (2020). *Poverty and Shared Prosperity 2020: Reversals of Fortune*. Washington, DC: World Bank.

World Economic Forum. (2015). *New Vision for Education: Unlocking the Potential of Technology*. Retrieved from http://www3.weforum.org/docs/WEFUSA_NewVisionforEducation_Report2015.pdf

World Economic Forum. (2016). *The Future of Jobs: Employment, Skills and Workforce Strategy for the Fourth Industrial Revolution*. Retrieved from http://www3.weforum.org/docs/WEF_Future_of_Jobs.pdf

World Health Organization (WHO). (1997). *Life Skills Education for Children and Adolescents in Schools*. Retrieved from https://www.who.int/publications/i/item/who-mnh-psf-93.7a

Wuthnow, R. (2002). Religious Involvement and Interfaith Service Projects: What Helps and What Hinders? *Nonprofit and Voluntary Sector Quarterly, 31*(3), 410-428.

Yao, X. (2000). *An Introduction to Confucianism*. Cambridge University Press.

Youniss, J., & Yates, M. (1997). *Community Service and Social Responsibility in Youth*. University of Chicago Press.

Yousafzai, M. (2013). *I Am Malala: The Girl Who Stood Up for Education and Was Shot by the Taliban*. Little, Brown and Company.

Yousafzai, M., & Lamb, C. (2013). *He Named Me Malala*. Little, Brown and Company.

Yousafzai, M., & McCormick, P. (2014). *Malala: My Story of Standing Up for Girls' Rights*. Little, Brown Books for Young Readers.

About The Author

Dr. Anton Anthony, Ed. S, ThD founder and creator of AA Steam & Entrepreneurship and the trademark pedagogy Steampreneurship has served in school districts throughout Georgia as a teacher, discipline coordinator, coach, assistant principal, principal, and district human resource professional.

He has worked in poverty-stricken schools where most of the population was Title I. He has also worked in schools where parents were highly educated, high-income professionals and business owners. Each school brought its own challenges, but he was able to break through barriers and achieve academic improvement everywhere he went.

Credentials
Dr. Anthony received his Bachelor of Arts with Honors in

Business Management from Fort Valley State University in Georgia. He received his Masters of Arts in Teaching at Augusta State University. He later returned to receive a degree in Curriculum and Instruction from Augusta University and received his Educational Specialist add-on in Educational Leadership and Administration, also at Augusta University. His Doctorate in Theology was awarded from North Central Theological Seminary. He is a licensed educator and real estate broker with the State of Georgia.

Career

He began his educational career as a reading specialist in Burke County, Georgia schools. He was moved into the 7th grade English/Language Arts program (ELA), where he experienced his first real taste of educational success. His class achieved the highest passing percentage, and he was given an award to recognize his achievement.

After spending a second year at the middle school where he began his career, he asked for a position as a coach at an alternative school in that same district. Former teacher of the year for the school, he was allowed to become the coach, discipline coordinator, and reading instructor. From those positions, he would become an assistant principal and principal.

Current Status

Mr. Anthony currently lives in Georgia. He is a resource professional for the 3rd largest school district in Georgia and looks forward to bringing his vision of AA STEAM & Entrepreneurship Academy to life.

Contact The Author

Contact Information
To connect with Mr. Anthony online, you can find him online.

Website
lovingeducation.org

Facebook: http://facebook.com/anton.anthony1
Twitter:
https://Twitter.com/antonanthony5

Instagram:
Instagram.com/oracle_of_education

LinkedIn:
www.linkedin.com/in/authorantonanthonysr

YouTube:
https://www.youtube.com/channel/UCI77nqy8OXItxQ_Zaz-NSmow

Email:
antonanthonysr@gmail.com

contact@lovingeducation.org

AAStemAcademy@gmail.com

Printed in the USA
CPSIA information can be obtained
at www.ICGtesting.com
LVHW022009160624
783318LV00001B/102